THE ABLE DIABETIC

LIFE FOOD

Disclaimer
This publication contains the opinions and ideas of its author. It is intended to provide helpful and informative material on the subjects addressed in the publication. It is not intended as and should not be relied upon as medical advice. It is sold with the understanding that the author and publisher are not engaged in rendering medical, health, or any other kind of medial or professional services in the book. The reader should consult his, her, or their medical, health, or other competent professional before adopting any of the suggestions in the book or drawing inferences from it. The author and publisher specifically disclaim all responsibility for any liability, loss, or risk, personal or otherwise, which is incurred as a consequence, directly or indirectly, of the use and applications of any of the contents of this book. If you have underlying health problems, or have any doubts about the information contained in this book, you should contact a qualified medical, dietary, or other appropriate professional.

Caution – discuss your diet plan with your doctor if any of the following apply:
You have a history of eating disorders
You are on insulin or a diabetic medication – you may need to plan how you change your medication if you undertake changes to your diet
You are on blood pressure tablets
You have moderate or severe retinopathy
You have a significant psychiatric disorder
You are taking warfarin
You have epilepsy
You have a significant medical condition

Published in 2025 by Sarah Harding

Copyright © Sarah Harding
Photographs © Sarah Harding

Page design and cover design by Sarah Harding

Sarah Harding has asserted her right under the Copyright, Designs and Patents Act 1988 to be identified as the author of this work. All rights reserved. No part of this publication may be reproduced, stored in a retrieval system or transmitted in any form, or by any means (electronic, mechanical, or otherwise) without the prior written permission of both the copyright owners and the publisher.

ISBN: 9798285371106

THE ABLE DIABETIC

LIFE FOOD

Food insight and recipes from
my type 1 diabetic life

Sarah Harding

Sarah Harding has been a type 1 diabetic since 1993. Being diabetic has not stopped her from living a full life. Her writing describes how she has managed to balance having a family, a fulfilling career, travel to all corners of the world, and an active lifestyle – in short to enjoy life to the full.

Managing food well is central to being in control as a diabetic. With all the usual challenges presented by busy lives, and modern food options, this isn't easy.

Having grappled with getting food choices right, not just personally but for feeding her family, and living life, this book describes how Sarah has adapted and managed.

It's practical, based on real life experience, and has lots of easy tips for choosing and making better food for diabetics.

For my family, Lauren, Greg and Jim,
with love and gratitude for being there
through the highs and lows of this diabetic life with me.

You are my everything.

CONTENTS

INTRODUCTION

MY OWN INSULIN REGIME AND DAILY PATTERN

NIBBLES

SOUPS

MAINS

SALADS

LIGHTER MEALS

BAKES

DESSERTS

A SPECIAL MENTION

LIFE FOOD

Introduction

Over more than thirty years of living with type 1 diabetes (t1d), I've learned a lot, through trial, error, reflection, and sheer persistence. Writing this book has been a way of gathering those lessons and insights into something useful: a practical, grounded guide for living well with t1d, through one of the biggest daily challenges we face, our food.

At the heart of it, this book is about balance. That word means something very specific to me: it's not just about nutrients or blood glucose levels, but about finding a way of living that works for me as an individual, with my own preferences, lifestyle, and values. There are broad principles that help make good choices and manage blood sugar effectively, but principles alone aren't enough. Life with t1d is lived in the details, the unpredictable moments and changing circumstances. That's where flexibility and being adaptable matter. It's where lived experience can help.

Managing food is a constant, complex challenge of living with t1d. Every single thing you eat has implications. It's not just about calculating insulin doses, but about weighing multiple, overlapping factors: nutrition, timing, activity, stress, family life, social plans. So many variables affect how food interacts with your body and your day. That means, meal by meal and hour by hour, you're assessing and adjusting.

I decided to write this cookbook when I noticed how much of my blog was about food, not just recipes, but the thought processes behind my choices. Writing about food became a way to reflect on how I've built a way of eating that supports both my blood sugar control and my broader life. I realised I was documenting the practical, sometimes invisible tweaks I make as a t1d: choosing one thing over another, adjusting portion sizes, balancing enjoyment with stability.

THE ABLE DIABETIC

I began thinking: what if I collected those recipes, the ones that have stood the test of time in our home, and shared them along with the thinking behind them? What if I could show how real meals, for real families, can be adapted to make life with t1d a bit easier?

That's the aim of this book. It's not glossy or idealised, it's practical and real. Food is hugely important to me, and I'll admit that this has often made life with t1d more difficult. I love good food. I love variety. I love the social side of meals and the comfort of family dinners. That makes the discipline t1d demands a little harder and it made it more essential that I found ways to make it work.

Planning meals helps me manage things. I sit down and write out 1 to 2 weeks of meals at a time, partly to stay on top of what we have already and reduce waste, but also to take a clear look at the balance: are we getting enough veg? Are there too many treats? Do I have what I need? That planning gives me a chance to get ahead of food choices before I'm standing in the kitchen, hungry and tired.

For t1ds, what we eat matters enormously. Ideally, meals should include plenty of veg and protein, both of which help slow down the digestion of carbohydrates and keep blood sugar more stable. Carb choices are especially important. High-fibre options help moderate the impact of a meal on blood glucose levels, and the total carb load needs to be carefully thought through. It takes time, knowledge, and experimentation to understand not only what foods contain, but how to modify or pair them for better outcomes. Add to that the unpredictability of life including work, kids, stress, illness, social events, and the challenge increases. For me, navigating that unpredictability is one of the hardest parts of staying in control.

Of course, the way I eat isn't just about diabetes but also about feeding a family. The recipes in this book reflect our values as a household: health, sustainability, enjoyment, and connection and have been adapted over time to meet both my health needs and the everyday demands of parenting, budgeting, and living well.

LIFE FOOD

My cooking is practical, frugal, and unapologetically homely. I care about avoiding waste, and constantly check what needs using up in the fridge. That's one reason why soups feature heavily: they're adaptable, healthy, and a great way to rescue odd bits and pieces. I focus on taste and sustenance, not style. This is food to be eaten, not admired. It's food for people with different preferences, ages, and demands, because that's real life.

We eat lots of fruit and veg, with an emphasis on the veg. Fruit is welcome, but because it affects blood sugar more quickly, it plays a smaller role. Pulses are a big feature of our meals: they're filling, affordable, and highly beneficial for blood glucose stability. That sets our diet apart from many others, but it's been a good shift for us.

Most of what we eat comes from supermarkets, not special shops. I don't use expensive or obscure ingredients. I make conscious choices, within a budget. When it comes to meat, we eat it, but not much. Good quality matters, especially when animals are involved. I do my best to buy meat and eggs from sources where animal welfare is taken seriously. Battery farming upsets me. I'd rather eat less meat and feel good about where it came from. The same values apply to sustainability. I try not to buy air-freighted produce and focus on seasonal, local food when I can. (Green beans, I love you, but if you're flown in from Kenya, sorry not for me.)

Writing this book has been a reflective and rewarding process. It's helped me clarify what matters to me, not just as a person with t1d, but as a parent, a cook, and someone trying to live well. If sharing these recipes and the thinking behind them helps others in a similar position, then I'm very happy.

Living with t1d involves a lot of thought, a huge number of small decisions, and a fair amount of discipline. But with a few steady habits and adaptations, I've found it's possible to live well and get loads out of life. Food is central to that for me, and I hope this book helps make it a little easier, a little tastier, and a little more satisfying for you too.

THE ABLE DIABETIC

LIFE FOOD

My own insulin regime and daily pattern

Everyone's experience of type 1 diabetes is different, and developing a rhythm that works for your own body and life is essential, not just for control, but for the sense life is being lived fully. So, in outlining how I do things, I'm not offering a model, just context. This is how I manage it.

I am on a basal-bolus regime. I take background insulin, Levemir, twice a day, once in the morning and once at bedtime. My current doses are 22 units in the morning and 12 at night. I also take fast-acting Humalog at meals and for corrections. A typical dose at a meal is between 5 and 13 units. For example, 5 units covers about one slice of bread, and 13 would be enough for two slices plus some extra carbohydrate, such as an apple. Bread is just a benchmark; I eat much more widely than that! Hopefully, it gives a helpful reference point.

Since 2016, I've used the Freestyle Libre continuous glucose monitor. Having a clear, immediate picture of what's happening with my blood sugar has transformed my ability to make decisions and respond in real time. I'm now much better equipped to understand how my body works, what's going on, and how to adapt accordingly.

One of the major changes I made, after several months of Libre data, was to stop eating breakfast. The medical advice I had previously was to eat three meals a day, but my data showed that my blood glucose stayed far more stable the longer I went without eating. So now, when I wake up, I take my usual background dose along with 2 units of Humalog, plus a little more if I'm higher than I'd like, and then I leave it there. I don't eat for several hours. That change has had a big positive effect on my overall profile.

My first meal is usually at lunchtime or in the early afternoon. I tend to keep it light, often a bowl of soup or a couple of eggs. Our main meal happens in the evening, which is when we sit down as a family.

THE ABLE DIABETIC

Work and school days dictate this is later than ideal, so despite the challenges for my blood sugar, we typically eat after 7pm.

Eating the biggest meal in the evening brings its difficulties. My glucose levels usually peak around 9 to 10 p.m. and are often high and possibly still peaking as I head to bed. When I first started using the Libre, I had to face the reality that it's rare for me to stay below 10 mmol/L after dinner. I'm often in the 12 to 15 mmol/L range. But if I try to avoid that rise, I tend to end up having a hypo once the peak passes, and often overnight.

In terms of dosing, I adjust my Humalog at every meal. For lunch or my first meal of the day, I usually take 5 to 8 units. For dinner, it's more, typically between 8 and 12 units. I've developed fairly accurate judgement for what I need, based on long experience and a lot of trial and error.

I also correct at other times, outside of meals. If I spot that my blood sugar is above 10 mmol/L and it's not just a post-meal peak, I'll take a small correction dose. As always, I factor in context, be it activity, stress, and all the other little variables that shape daily life.

This way of managing isn't perfect, but it works for me. It's flexible, responsive, and based on real life. It reflects not only what I've learned over time, but also the value of choosing stability and sustainability over chasing ideal numbers. Like the rest of my approach to living with type 1 diabetes, it's about making space for life, not just for control.

NIBBLES

NIBBLES

Roasted nuts

Crudites

Hummus

Bloody Mary tomatoes

Filo carrots

Antipasti

LIFE FOOD

The very concept of nibbling isn't diabetic-friendly. Eating in a randomised fashion is opposed to good diabetic principles of eating with control and precision. And eating carbs, however seemingly trivial shouldn't generally happen without taking some insulin. Determining the correct insulin dose when you're going to be grazing is a real challenge because it is so unpredictable and also not something you do every day. However, sometimes in life you are faced with a situation where you have to navigate 'small food'.

Nibbling and social situations seem to go hand in hand, and are the hardest part of navigating food as a t1d in my view. A key point is that grazing means you can't guarantee you're going to have enough to eat to match your dose, and you also can't guarantee that you won't accidentally overdo it.

Often, the situations where I am nibbling are ones where alcohol is involved too. The combination of ad hoc food and drinking is one which carries a real risk I'll often get it wrong, with resulting blood sugars either too low or too high.

It's an important note that in drinking situations with minimal food, the chance of having a hypo is heightened, so always ensure you have something sugary to eat if needed, and be alert to hypo symptoms that you might put down to the alcohol.

I have found over time that despite the challenges there is a place in my life for nibbles. And I am all about living life. I don't want to miss out on socialising with friends and not have a few bites of some canapés when I'm relaxing and enjoying that moment.

My approach is to be selective wherever possible and gravitate to low-carb options, trying to avoid taking much insulin at all. When I'm eating at a level that involves injecting only about a quarter to a third of a meal dose, I can stay in a fairly safe zone. That little insulin doesn't allow me to eat much carbohydrate though. It's a delicate balance.

THE ABLE DIABETIC

There are foods that are much better than others. Some things that are often laid out for grazing aren't great at all, like breadsticks, crisps, and tortilla chips, which are all very high carb. If you start on these, quickly you'll find you're eating way more carbs than you should. Much better are low glycaemic index (GI) vegetable based or protein based things.

Foods I would say yes to in a grazing situation would include skewers of meat, olives, meat or fish goujons, prawns (yes to mayo based dip), cocktail sausages, devilled eggs, and cubed cheese. All of these have minimal carbs.

Things I would avoid would include things served on slices of toasted bread, mini burgers, mini quiches, samosas or pakoras, mini pizzas, bruschetta, blinis, potato skins, pastry pinwheels, sausage rolls.

You get the idea.

At home, we don't do a lot on nibbling, which now I reflect, is probably down to me! We do have a sharing bag of crisps from time to time, which is primarily intended for the rest of the family, and would be a Friday night thing. Yes, I would have some. Is that good? No, my blood sugars will go up. From a life point of view though, a little out of control sometimes is ok as long as most of the time I'm in target. I'd correct this as part of the meal insulin dosage that would follow soon.

It is useful to know what to provide as a host if you need some food that will go alongside drinks with friends that will be easier for a t1d to enjoy as part of the event. The ideas given here are easy and enjoyable ways to consider diabetics when eating in a casual way.

LIFE FOOD

THE ABLE DIABETIC

LIFE FOOD

Roasted nuts

Nuts have a lot going for them. I think it is generally helpful to think of food in terms of its nutrition rather than restriction. That sounds quite obvious until you consider how many other roles food has: as a lifestyle thing, as entertainment, as fuel, as a treat, and less positively as about dieting, calorie restriction, and something to worry about. While people try to eat healthily overall, the consideration of an item, and its inherent nutrition is not often front of mind. Nuts, in their original form, without the addition of sugary stuff or salt, are super-nutritious, containing great fats, protein and a degree of carbs plus vitamins and minerals.

Often, nuts as a snack are out of a packet and have been coated in sugary, salty, fatty extras. I would encourage home roasting nuts for a much healthier nibble without any of the added and unnecessary extras. Freshly roasted nuts are delicious on their own.

You need a good mixture of different kinds of nuts, of whatever type you like! Different nuts will take a different amount of roasting. At the shorter end are walnuts, pecans, pistachios and cashews and at the longer end, almonds and hazelnuts.

You just lay them out in a roasting tray, put them in an oven at 170° C / 340° F / Gas mark 3, and roast for between 8 and 13 minutes. Every 2-3 minutes they need getting out and jigging around to turn them for an even roast.

Keep an eye on them because overdoing it is not what you want. They aren't that forgiving if you forget them, and burnt nuts are not appetising!

Personally, I think these are perfect with an early evening aperitif, something you don't need a lot of but just makes the drink into something special.

Crudites

Crudites are an option that always under-promise and over-deliver, which is a rare and wonderful thing in life! I always think that a pile of chopped veg sounds incredibly boring, and yet, it absolutely isn't. With no trouble at all, you can create a plateful of colour, interest, and good health. Putting this in front of children, and adults who would prefer crisps, works.

Prep as close to eating as you can. I once saw on TV someone give their child a cut up carrot instead of pre-prepared carrots sticks out of a plastic bag and the child was ecstatic at how much nicer the fresh carrot stick was. Absolutely! Vegetables are far nicer if they are freshly cut, crisp and crunchy.

The quantities here are completely in your control. The amount for one person is different to the amount to make for a party. I'm sure you can work it out!

Ingredients

All of the vegetables need to be well washed before prepping.
- Cherry tomatoes – as they are.
- Cucumber – cut into 5cm lengths, the squishy middle cut out, and then cut into thin sticks.
- Carrots – peeled, topped and tailed, cut into 5cm chunks and then slices into thin sticks.
- Celery – end trimmed, cut into 5cm lengths, and then into thin slices.
- Cauliflower, with the florets cut off and into bite sized pieces.
- Red, orange and yellow peppers, remove seeds and stalk, cut into slices.
- Button mushrooms – trim the stalks, and either serve as they are, or cut into halves.
- Radishes – topped, tailed and halved.

- Little gem leaves – separated into individual leaves and cut length ways if too large.

<u>Method</u>

Cut the vegetables up, and lay out on a platter or board attractively.

Refrigerate if you are serving in more than an hour from prep time.

And do cover them in between prep and eating.

Hummus

My go to accompaniment for crudites is a kind of beginners' level hummus. It's something that takes approximately 4 minutes to whip up, uses store cupboard ingredients, and has healthy carbs and protein in it to boot. I don't usually use tahini, which is a traditional ingredient, and I do often add something 'extra': a bit of smoked paprika, or cumin, or chilli flakes.

Real hummus recipes tend to add quite a lot of oil as well as the tahini, probably partly because the tahini texture can be quite hard, needing the oil to loosen it. It tastes lovely, and you get a fab silky texture if you add more oil than I do, but it seems unnecessary to me, and so I reduce the amount. It is intentional, and if you compare my recipe to others, you're entitled to conclude that mine isn't that authentic.

I'm into the hummus for its pulse based goodness and its yumminess.

Ingredients

1 400g tin chickpeas, drained and rinsed
2 cloves garlic, paper skins removed
1 lemon, juiced
A good pinch salt
50ml of olive oil

Method

I use a handheld stick blender for this, and assemble the ingredients in the special cup that goes with it. Just as easily you can use a food processor.

Put the chickpeas, cloves of garlic, lemon juice, salt and olive oil in what you're using to process them, and pulse. If the mixture is too

LIFE FOOD

dry add water bit by bit and continue to pulse. Whiz it all until it is smooth.

Decant into a bowl, and drizzle with a little more olive oil.

N.B. If you want to add paprika, cumin, or chilli – all of which are popular in our household, add half a teaspoon before you start the whizzing.

Bloody Mary tomatoes

My friend Sarah made this for a party and based as it is on a Bloody Mary cocktail, what's not to like?! The tomatoes are piquant and have a kind of double kick, both spicy and from the alcohol. Making it is simple, although I found a bit of practice to get exactly the right taste necessitated some 'practice makes perfect' experiments. I find that being over-generous with the seasonings is a good thing, but it is a lot easier to add seasoning than to take it away so be a bit careful!

From my t1d perspective, these are wonderful to have at a party. They have no impact on my blood sugars because they are super low carb, and because they are a small mouthful, they also aren't very alcoholic. So, the spot they occupy is a blissfully easy one. They are right at the top of things that I feel relaxed about. And yet, they are fun and tasty, perfect for something low impact but smart and fab all at the same time.

These are served as nibbles so cater according to the size of your party! The amount below is typically what I'd make for a few friends.

Ingredients

Cherry tomatoes – 2 punnets (make more if you want!)
Celery salt – 1 teaspoon
Vodka – 150ml
Worcestershire sauce – generous splash

Method

You need to prepare these at least 8 hours before you want to serve them. Preparation is super simple.

Get a glass or other non-reactive dish which will accommodate the tomatoes in one layer. This is key – the cherry tomatoes have to be in contact with the liquid.

LIFE FOOD

In a glass mix up the vodka, celery salt, and Worcestershire sauce, and stir to dissolve the salt, then pour into the glass dish.

Wash the cherry tomatoes. Then for each one, using a sharp knife, cut a cross across the top of the cherry tomato where it was attached to the stalk. The incision needs to be a couple of millimetres deep.

Place the cherry tomatoes so that the crosses are in the vodka mixture. Then pop in the fridge and chill while the tomatoes absorb the vodka which they will do over a number of hours.

To serve, take the cherry tomatoes out of the vodka, which will hopefully mainly have been sucked up into the fruit, and dry on some kitchen towel. Then put them on a serving plate with the crosses upright.

THE ABLE DIABETIC

Filo carrots

Carrots. So basic as to be ignored in favour of more interesting and exotic things. Not in my world. I lament the short shrift this amazing, prolific, cheap, nutritious vegetable gets. There are a lot of delicious things that you can make from some carrots.

These carrot 'cigars' are surprisingly elegant, and moreish. They are lightly wrapped in filo, nicely spiced, and made into lovely, crunchy, tasty nibbles.

Filo pastry is a gift for diabetics. Because it is so thin and delicate, it doesn't add too much in the way of carbs for all manner of 'pie' and 'wrapped' recipes, but it is effective at doing the parcelling job that pastry is often there for. It also elevates something simple into something that feels like there is some effort going on here. I also like that sprinkled with a few seeds it looks especially pretty.

Some people think filo is a faff to use, and it's true that allowing it to dry out creates insuperable problems, so you need to work fast with it, but a little bit of practice is all you need. No need to be nervous. (I give detailed instructions on how to use filo pastry in the recipe for Salmon and Broccoli filo quiche in the Mains section, so have a read of that if you're not confident).

Keep the open filo, in its oblong pile, covered in a clean, damp tea towel, and be all set up with a pastry brush and oil and melted butter mixture so that you can move fast.

Ingredients
500g carrots (about 7 medium carrots)
6-7 sheets of filo pastry (typically half a packet)
30 mls sunflower oil + 20g melted butter mixed together
2 teaspoons cumin seeds

LIFE FOOD

Method

Preheat the oven to 180° C / 350° F / Gas mark 4.

Peel, top and tail your carrots, and if medium sized, cut into quarters along the length of the carrot, and in half through the middle. You should end up with about 50 batons.

Get the filo pastry out and unfold it, then cover it with a damp clean tea towel. Take out 1 sheet, and brush the entire sheet with the sunflower and melted butter mixture. Then cut the sheet of filo in half lengthways, and into four widthways – you should now have 8 pieces of filo. Take each piece and wrap the carrot in it. Lay on a baking tray.

Keep going until you have done all the carrots, which will use 2 or 3 baking trays depending on how big they are. Sprinkle the cumin seeds over the carrots.

Put the baking trays into the oven and cook for 30 minutes. The filo should be golden brown.

Allow to cool so they are warm before transferring to a plate to serve.

THE ABLE DIABETIC

Antipasti

I'm a big fan of food offerings that allow people (whoever they are) to self-select food. As a diabetic, I'm used to sizing up the options and making decisions based on a number of factors. An antipasti board is an ideal way of giving me those options.

We often have this on a Friday night at home. 'Friday Night is Pizza Night' was a cornerstone of family life as the children were growing up. I loved it because it was easy at the end of a long work week. The children loved pizza. But it was a bit of a disaster of a diabetic meal. You can't get away from its carb-heaviness, and so it always involved a lot more insulin than other meals, and as I got older, that got harder for me. Also, I usually have a couple of glasses of wine on a Friday night, and that led to over-indulging in pizza. Bad.

Part of the reason I'm writing this book is to show how my own choices have developed, and what I'm thinking about as I plan food. The pizza night is a lot easier if it is combined with other things, and that's where the antipasti approach came from.

I would usually do 4 of the following, alongside a pizza. The antipasti bits should be selected to limit the number of fatty options, and so that you end up with vegetables in the mix – it's about creating balance.

- Always a green salad, lettuce or spinach, or a rocket & parmesan salad is there.
- Tomato, avocado, mozzarella salad with basil (almost always served).
- Roasted red peppers.
- Roasted aubergine slices.
- A mixed bean salad
- Button mushrooms, cooked in the oven with garlic and some butter and herbs.
- A platter of salamis.
- Artichokes from a jar, well drained of their oil

LIFE FOOD

- Greek salad: cucumber, tomato, red onion, black olives, a little feta, dressed in olive oil, lemon juice and sprinkled with oregano.
- Olives, green or black.
- Tuna and cannellini beans, with some sliced red onion.
- A luxurious treat – burrata and roasted peaches.

Suddenly my plate can have a slice of pizza, plenty of lettuce, and a couple of other delicious and lower-carb options, and everything is good.

SOUPS

SOUPS

Lentil and apricot soup

Broccoli and cannellini bean soup

Bacon and lentil soup

Minestrone soup

Curried split pea soup

Mexican bean soup

Turkish red lentil soup

Borscht

Smoked haddock and sweetcorn chowder

Pho

LIFE FOOD

Soups are a constant feature of my cooking, especially in the colder months of the year. This is because they are so readily adaptable, and I can personalise them to meet my own needs.

Core to this is that soups are a great vehicle for vegetables of every kind, and they also lend themselves to including pulses, again of every kind. Basing a meal around veg and pulses means that I am halfway to a perfect meal. That statement would apply to everyone, not just diabetics, but as a t1d I find this core combination is central to the best food for me.

For type 1 diabetics, pulses are superfoods. There is a strong theme throughout this book of my adding pulses wherever I can. While I was already using red lentils when I was diagnosed in 1993, I have gradually extended that to use any type of pulse I can find. I enjoy the variety, and feel that despite my food often having a pulse element, it's not too samey if lots of different kinds are used. I find it makes a marked difference to my blood sugar profile after a meal if I've used pulses to replace bread, pasta and rice. The reason for this is replacing refined carbs like pasta, bread, and rice with pulses results in the much-slower release of carbs, lower carb content overall, and extra fibre. These things combined with additional protein all drive benefits to my blood sugar control and overall health.

The soups I make are generally pretty hearty because I intend for them to be a complete meal. I enjoy the variety of chunky or smooth, soothing or spiky, simple or complex, rustic or refined. But however they are presented, I will usually incorporate healthy carbs from either pulses or the variety of vegetable used, and so these soups do need me to take insulin. Even without bread they are a meal.

I have a few soups that come round often, such as minestrone, and the curried split pea soup, but while I stick to a generally recognisable recipe, the way I cook means there will almost always be some tweaks. I'll add a few chunks of some vegetable that is lurking around without a use. This kind of cooking is friendly and accommodating - it'll take on most things.

I also make stock, or as it has become fashionably known, bone broth. For a long time, this has been something I've embraced because I care about the animal we're eating. In the case of chicken, we rarely eat chicken that isn't a whole chicken, and it has to be a blue moon for chicken breasts to come into our home. Whenever we have chicken, I always boil up the carcass or bones afterwards to make stock. I actually find it quite hard to use up all the stock I make, despite a chicken only coming round every 2-3 weeks, and so we always have it in the freezer. It's another reason why soup works so well for us! And I'm not joking when I say that I think there is turkey stock from the Christmas before last in the depths of the freezer – I'm sure there is! Also, stock contains lots of protein, so with veg, pulses, and stock you really do have the components of a highly nutritious and enjoyable meal.

The last thing I'll say on this is that soup lends itself to sitting in the fridge or being batched and frozen, and this too is a factor I find useful. Life is busy and our household like many others revolves around a quick sandwich or a couple of slices of toast if there isn't another easy option on standby. That's not good for me. So, from a practical point of view, if I make a big batch of soup at the weekend, I'm covered through the week for lunch. Being prepared with healthy options helps a lot with the task of eating well as a t1d on a constant, everyday basis.

LIFE FOOD

THE ABLE DIABETIC

LIFE FOOD

Lentil and apricot soup

It is downright mind blowing that tiny, seemingly inconsequential, things can have a lifelong impact. Back before I was diagnosed with my type 1 diabetes, a year before in fact, I got into lentils and brown rice because in preparation for going to live in a shared house at uni, my dad bought me a cash & carry size bag of brown rice and a humungous bag of orange split lentils. I remember him kind of suggesting this was a good idea and me looking at the vast quantity and thinking it was completely mad, but just going along with it.

What do you do when faced with about 5 kilos of rice and lentils?!

There was no google back then, but a Delia cookbook at home gave me a couple of recipes I read and then made my own. One was a brown rice and spinach bake – my version is later in the book, and I include my bacon and lentil soup later in this section.

I also tried to make dhal, a major failure initially, and something I didn't come back to for at least a decade, but it too is in this book in the Mains section.

While Delia's recipe did not use red lentils, so I was freestyling from the start, the bacon and lentil soup was a real success, and established in me a relationship with lentils that meant that after I had eventually worked through the first sack, I bought them myself! It wasn't until I was in my thirties that I branched out and discovered lentils could be in so many things. They became such stalwarts of my kitchen, that it was important that they were always available.

That original bag of lentils was red lentils. Red lentils are very cool because they cook so quickly. Within 20 minutes start to finish you can have a lentil soup from nothing. When I came across this recipe, I've forgotten where, I immediately knew it would be a good one. Red lentils love warm spice. They also love something sweet as a foil against them, which the apricots provide. This couldn't be simpler or more enjoyable.

THE ABLE DIABETIC

Serves 4

<u>Ingredients</u>

Glug of sunflower oil
1 onion
2 cloves garlic
1 teaspoon red birds' eye chilli / ½ teaspoon of chilli flakes or powder
150g red lentils
1 pint of stock (can be chicken, vegetable, whatever you want as long as it's something light)
12 dried apricots
Squeeze of lemon
Greek yogurt (or other plain) to serve

<u>Method</u>
In a large saucepan, warm a dollop of sunflower oil. Chop the onion up finely and add to the oil, then gently fry for a few minutes, until it is slightly browned, but only just.

Meanwhile, put the red lentils in a sieve and wash under running water.

Crush the garlic cloves, chop the chilli / and add them to the pan, and let cook for a minute or so, and then pour in the stock. Add the red lentils. Bring the whole thing to a gentle simmer.

Roughly chop the dried apricots up and add them to the pan. (This soup is going to be blended which is why they are chopped roughly, but the soup is perfectly fine, just a bit more textured, if it's not blended. If you are going to skip the blending, I would recommend chopping the apricots up finely).

Watch the pot from time to time while it's cooking, and add boiling water (from a kettle) if it is too dry. After 25 minutes, the lentils will be falling-apart soft. If they aren't, give them a bit longer. Add more water if needed too.

Then blend. I use a hand blender, straight into the saucepan, and whizz it up until the soup is smooth. Add the lemon juice. This makes the whole thing sing.

Serve in deep bowls, with a generous swirl of Greek yogurt.

N.B., I also make this with half a can of coconut milk added at the final stage (and dispense with the yogurt). If I do this, I like to add a bit more spice: cumin, coriander, ginger, as well as the chilli and garlic.

THE ABLE DIABETIC

Broccoli and cannellini bean soup

This soup was the third I shared on my blog, and so was right at the start of my thinking that sharing my approach to food could be useful.

The origins of this recipe are way back to my twenties when I picked up how to make broccoli and cheddar soup from a recipe card in a magazine. That's all I can recall so am not sure which chef's name should be credited! I've included it here because aside from being yum it's also a good example of how food can be adjusted to be more diabetically friendly.

I've made a few key changes. The first is that I've increased the amount of broccoli – I use the whole thing, including stems, with the woody bits cut off. The original recipe used 1 large potato, and I have replaced this with a tin of cannellini beans, because that way there's a better carb profile and you get the legume protein and fibre to boost. The third change is to not add cream. I'm not suggesting that it's not nice to have cream but it's not necessary and the beans add extra creaminess to the texture anyway. Lastly, I do tend to garnish with a little cheese and rather than cheddar I prefer stilton.

All of these changes make this a straightforward and delicious meal for a t1d (and everyone else).

Serves 4

Ingredients

Glug sunflower oil
1 onion
1 head broccoli
1 litre light stock
1 400g tin cannellini beans, drained
50g stilton, crumbled

LIFE FOOD

<u>Method</u>

In a large saucepan, put a chopped onion and a little sunflower oil and lightly sauté for a few minutes without it getting to the brown stage.

Prepare the broccoli by separating off the florets and cutting into quite small pieces and then chopping the rest up. Keep these two piles separate!

Once the onion has reached the translucent stage add the stock and the 'stem' pile of chopped broccoli. Simmer this until the pieces are not yet cooked, they give some resistance, but are about ¾ of the way there.

At this point add the drained cannellini beans and the rest of the broccoli i.e., the florets. Timing gets quite key now as the objective is to cook the florets until they are still bright green but just cooked. Once that cooked stage has been reached quickly blend the soup until smooth. I like it well blended but with just a smidgen left of the texture.

Serve immediately, with crumbled stilton (or grated cheddar) on top if you wish. By the way, I don't add salt and pepper as I'm cooking this and with the cheese, I think salt is unnecessary, but a bit of white pepper is welcome.

Very pretty and very delicious!

Bacon and lentil soup

My lentil story is told above, and I owe Delia's smoked bacon and lentil soup a huge amount. I have eaten innumerable versions of it countless times over 3 decades. Delia makes it clear that the soup is best made with whole green-brown lentils, and I eventually got into using those regularly. But my first efforts used the original red lentils and gave an orangey looking soup with bits of green savoy cabbage to contrast. It was perfectly good.

When I got older and brought the brown-green lentils into the mix, I still used a mixture of the red and green, liking the texture the red ones gave. And by then, my soup was my soup, and Delia's a fond but distant memory!

A couple of health and food-choice related points. Much as I love bacon, it increasingly makes a rare appearance in my food, because it's not known for being a health food, being fatty and quite processed, and also the wellbeing of the pigs matters a lot to me, so I am completely averse to buying unhappy pig meat. Consequently, this soup often gets made when I have a couple of rashers left over from something else. One packet of bacon becomes 3 meals in my home. It is lovely to have the smoky flavour of bacon in this soup though and makes it what it is. The other health point is the savoy cabbage. Its leaves, especially the dark ones, contain loads of goodness, and so you're giving an important extra dimension by including them, even though they do feel, at the point you add them, like they're not that necessary!

Again, this is a perfect t1d lunch food, and with some bread on the side makes for a wonderful 'dinner' meal too.

Serves 4

Ingredients

Glug of sunflower oil

LIFE FOOD

1 onion
2 sticks of celery
1 large carrot
3 cloves of garlic
75g smoked bacon, chopped up small
400g tin of chopped tomatoes
1 pint of stock (chicken, vegetable)
200g of mixed red lentils & green lentils
40g tiny pasta shapes or broken up spaghetti
200g shredded savoy cabbage
Glug extra virgin olive oil
Salt & pepper

Method
Start with a large saucepan on the hob, with a good glug of sunflower oil. Finely dice the onion, celery, and carrot, and add to the pan. Cook over a medium heat for a few minutes until soft. I leave the pan lid on for this, and part steam the veg too.

Add the chopped bacon, and continue to fry for a few minutes, until it is giving its own fat out, and is looking quite cooked.

Add the chopped tomatoes, the stock, and the lentils, and pop the lid back on. Let this all simmer for about 40 minutes, checking in on it from time to time to check it hasn't run out of stock, and is bubbling happily. Check the green lentils' level of cooking completion by squidging one or two and when they are not hard the soup is close to ready.

10 minutes before you want to eat the soup, add the small pasta pieces, and the shredded savoy. You may need to add a bit more water at this point, in which case do.

This soup is served as it comes, so not blended. Serve in deep bowls, and garnish with a dash of olive oil sprinkled on top, and salt and pepper on the side.

THE ABLE DIABETIC

Minestrone soup

Simply due to the fact that this has spaghetti in it, this soup if my son's favourite. It's hilarious that just that fact moves a soup based on vegetables into the 'great food' category! Win-win though. I love how easy, cheap, and nutritious this is. He loves it for his own reason. Bril.

There is no such thing as a definitive minestrone recipe, as with anything made over generations by frugal mums and grandmas in countless kitchens. The recipe below is what I consider the basic soup, and it can be added to with lots of different veg. I would suggest not overloading it with any one thing; it's minestrone when the basic soup is still there after you've added a few of your own ideas. If you go too heavy with any other ingredient it becomes x-ingredient-vegetable-and pasta-soup. A bit of a balance!

The olive oil is essential here too. A good glug of olive oil to finish the soup, just before serving is something that lifts the whole thing.

I like to serve this with my own garlic bread which I make with malted granary bread, bought unsliced, sliced thickly, slathered with garlic butter and cooked in the oven for a few minutes before serving the soup. This does make the soup equal to a proper meal, and I will take a full meal dose of insulin if I have bread on the side. Of course, this is a substantial enough soup that it definitely serves well on its own as a good lunch.

Serves 4

Ingredients

Glug sunflower oil
1 onion
2 sticks of celery
1 large carrot
3 cloves garlic

LIFE FOOD

1 400g tin cannellini or borlotti beans
1 400g tin of chopped tomatoes
1 pint of chicken or vegetable stock
100g broken up spaghetti / pasta bits
Plus, 400g of extra mixed vegetables such as courgettes, leeks, sweet potato, spinach, butternut squash, peas (I do not recommend brassicas though so avoid broccoli, cauliflower, and also mushrooms change the nature of the soup too much).
Extra virgin olive oil to serve
Parmesan / other hard cheese, grated

Method

Make the soup in a large saucepan.

Chop the onion, celery and carrot into fine dice. Put the pan on the heat, add the sunflower oil, and put the onion, celery and carrot mix into the pan, and gently cook over a medium heat for a few minutes, about 3-5.

Then crush the garlic, add to the pan, and move around for another minute or so, and add the tomatoes and stock. Drain and rinse the beans in the tin, and add to the soup liquid in the pan. Bring to a simmer.

Meanwhile, prepare the other veg, by cleaning and peeling them where necessary, and chopping into small pieces, typically 0.5cm-1cm wide. Once chopped, add to the simmering saucepan. Cook the soup for 30 minutes.

Minestrone benefits from the character that it will develop with both slow, lengthy cooking, and also being cooled and then reheated. Whatever continues to go on when the thing is given space and time does make a difference to the flavour and texture. And often this is what I will do. But, in terms of getting a meal done from start to finish, the 30 minutes of basic cooking is what you actually need to do.

THE ABLE DIABETIC

10 minutes before the soup is to be served, add the broken spaghetti / pasta bits, more hot boiled water if needed, and cook for 10 minutes.

Serve the soup in bowls with a drizzle of olive oil on top, grated parmesan or similar, and salt & pepper on the side for people to make it perfect for their own taste.

LIFE FOOD

Curried split pea soup

This is a proper meal-in-a-bowl, a warming, sustaining soup that I think brings a glow on the most grey and wintry of days.

This soup is thick with pulses and as a result there is a lot of carbs in it. They're good carbs, and will release slowly, but personally I would not add bread on the side here.

This soup is profoundly yellow, from both the turmeric and the yellow split peas. I am intentional about the yellow, because I find it inviting and appealing. It has a kind of deep, ochre-y quality. Turmeric is a great spice to add to food, bringing a range of health benefits, including that it is anti-inflammatory, and has nutrients that protect the body by neutralising free radicals which are damaging molecules. Lots of people take turmeric as a supplement. I don't subscribe to the whole supplement thing, preferring to focus on eating well and healthily to get what you need.

The great majority of my food has its roots in cultures from across the world. I've been fortunate to have travelled a lot in my life, and am always keen to taste new things. This soup isn't from anywhere specific, but it certainly reflects influences from Asia, the Middle East and northern Africa. It's a source of pleasure for me that food has the power to connect us.

The yellow split peas do not need special treatment (some pulses do) and so you can make this from start to finish in about an hour. I try to remember to soak the split peas however because it reduces the cooking time and saves energy. As a no-effort hack that contributes, even if just a little, to overall energy use, it seems like a no brainer to me.

Serves 4

Ingredients
Glug sunflower oil

THE ABLE DIABETIC

1 onion
3 cloves garlic
2 teaspoons turmeric
1 teaspoon medium chilli powder
200g yellow split peas
1 pint of stock / stock cube (chicken / vegetable)
salt

Greek yogurt to serve

<u>Method</u>

Get a large saucepan and put to warm on the hob, and add the glug of sunflower oil, and the onion – chopped into small dice. Cook over a medium heat for 3-4 minutes, stirring around from time to time.

Crush the garlic and add to the pan with the turmeric and the chilli, and continue to stir for a minute.

Pour on the stock, and bring to a simmer. Then, after rinsing the yellow split peas in a sieve, put them in the pot too. Leave this on a gentle simmer with the saucepan lid on, for about 45m to an hour, ensuring that the water is topped up if needed. Stir occasionally to make sure that the split peas don't stick to the bottom of the pan as then they'll burn. As they get softer and closer to disintegrating the chances increase so do keep an eye on things.

The soup is cooked when the split peas are at the point of disintegrating or when you squish them, and they are fully squishable.

Blend the soup with a hand blender or in a food processor, to smooth. The texture will still be 'pulse-y', but it's quite a lot more refined than if you don't blend. I check the taste and add a little salt at this point.

LIFE FOOD

Best served in rustic, deep bowls.

I do like the Greek yogurt swirled on top to serve – the texture and heat of the soup against the smoothness and coldness of the yogurt are lovely.

Mexican bean soup

This soup is based upon one that I used to buy from a supermarket, and although I was a big fan of it, the amount of plastic waste for 2 portions just upset me so much that I worked out I could make something similar myself and with minimal eco-impact. My enthusiasm for anything legume-based leading the way again too!

One of my favourite gadgets is a Thermos soup flask. I've had mine for yonks, and it is awesome. In the colder parts of the year as I get ready to go to work in the office, I heat up a portion of my soup (already made and in fridge) in the morning and decant it into the soup flask. It is still hot at lunchtime and makes a much better lunch than sandwiches. I highly recommend it.

Having the beans in this soup means that there are carbs within it. Not much, so if I were to eat this soup as it is I would need a small amount of insulin, which is ideal if this is lunch for me, or if I want something more substantial, I will add some bread on the side, and increase the insulin. I find the fact that this is a low impact meal diabetically valuable.

If you would like the soup to be more substantial, you can add 50g-100g of red lentils when the tomatoes and stock is added and you'll get something more substantial and higher carb, but still a great meal. Anyway, here's the recipe.

Serves 4

Ingredients

Glug sunflower oil
1 onion
1 stick celery
1 large carrot
3 cloves garlic
Good teaspoon Smoked paprika

LIFE FOOD

Good teaspoon cumin
½ teaspoon chilli flakes
2 red peppers
400g tin tomatoes
Stock (chicken, vegetable)
400g tin kidney or black beans, drained and rinsed

Method

In a large saucepan, warm the sunflower oil. Chop the onion and the celery into small dice and add to the oil. Cut the carrot into slightly larger dice. Lightly fry for a few minutes until the vegetables are soft, and slightly browning. Then add the garlic, smoked paprika, cumin and chili flakes, and briefly cook too.

Prepare the red peppers by deseeding, and chop into 1cm square pieces. The size here is dictated by the fact this is soup and you'll be eating the bits off a spoon! Put them in the saucepan, and pour in the tin of tomatoes, followed by the stock. Bring to a simmer, and let the soup cook for 20 minutes or so. Add the beans, and warm them through.

The soup is ready (that was quick) and will be quite happy to be saved and reheated or eaten straight away.

Turkish red lentil soup

Over the years, any recipe that contains red lentils which has crossed my path has been picked up and considered. This one had a lot of attributes that I like. It immediately sounds spicy, warming, a great use of not a lot of meat, and sustaining. It is gorgeous. It also feels authentic. Transports you to a place where it is outdoors, sunny, and there's a babble of homely welcoming in the air. I'm feel warm just thinking about Turkey and its people.

This is a soup that somehow spans the seasons too. In my mind most soups 'belong' somewhere in the rhythm of the year, driven be the seasonality of the produce, or the fact that they are 'hearty' (winter) or 'fresh' (summer). This recipe suits both. It manages to be both filling, and also completely at home eaten in the garden on a summer's day.

This is nice served with warm pitta bread, and my son likes it when there is hummus on the side with them too. A swirl of thick plain yogurt is also a lovely addition.

Ingredients

Glug sunflower oil
1 onion, diced
1 carrot, diced finely
4 cloves garlic, peeled and crushed
1 ½ teaspoon cumin
1 teaspoon coriander (ground)
½ - 1 teaspoon chilli powder
250g lamb mince
Tomato puree, a few teaspoons
120g red split lentils - rinsed
2 litres chicken stock
Mint leaves (especially in summer)

LIFE FOOD

<u>Method</u>

This is super easy to make. You need a large saucepan that will take the volume (so 3 litres is ideal), on a medium heat on the hob, into which put a small glug of the sunflower oil just to get things started. Go easy on the oil, because the lamb contains fat. Add the onion and carrot and sauté for a minute or so, then add the garlic and spices, cook for 1 minute, then add the mince and cook it, stirring it frequently, until it is browned.

Be ready with the hot stock, and pour into the pan, adding the tomato puree, and the red lentils. Then get it to a low simmer, with the lid on, and leave for 25 minutes.

This is one of those meals that benefits from cooking slowly, over a bit more time, so if you have it, I recommend that you let time work its magic. The red lentils should get to a point where they are disintegrating, and thickening the soup.

While the soup is cooking, wash the mint and pick the leaves off the stems. Discard the stems. Lightly chop the mint. When you're ready to eat, put the soup in bowls and sprinkle the mint on top.

THE ABLE DIABETIC

Borscht

One of the saddest things of recent years has been the war in Ukraine. I worked for a company that owned a Ukrainian broadcaster and between 2004 and 2008, visited Kyiv often, where their offices were right in the centre of town. They overlooked Independence Square, where Orange Revolution demonstrations took place. Because the people I worked with were in the TV industry there was a lot of passion for freedom of expression. The hotel I habitually stayed in, the Premier Palace Hotel, was lovely: Ukrainian in being very hospitable. The menu wasn't extensive, but was good quality, and included Chicken Kyiv, which always made me smile, pierogi dumplings, and that other classic, borscht. I'd never tasted it before then, and I loved it when I tried it.

This kind of soup is not, as I understand it, Ukrainian, but more likely Polish, and from the whole of this region. The name Borscht is actually Russian. I'm not going to get hung up on the labels.

I am going to spare a moment to think about the people suffering from the effects of a terrible war.

Anything that has such an amazing, vibrant colour is almost guaranteed to be good for you. The colour of beetroots indicates a wealth of antioxidants which support general good health. Beetroots have a low glycaemic index, and are high in fibre. They also contain anti-inflammatory properties, and nitrates which have a positive effect on blood pressure. So not only an unusual and quite exotic soup, but an excellent choice for us t1ds.

Adding vinegar to soup is not something I usually do, but Borscht has both a richness, and earthiness to it, and also a distinct tang. There are more authentic ways to bring that tang to bear which involves some kind of fermentation activity. I don't stretch to that kind of dedication, and the vinegar works well, so I do recommend it.

LIFE FOOD

Here's the version that I make myself, an amalgamation of other recipes and my memories.

Serves 4 - 6

<u>Ingredients</u>
Glug of sunflower oil
20g butter
1 onion, diced finely
1 stick celery, chopped
1 carrot, peeling and chopped
3 garlic cloves, crushed
1 bay leaf
1.5 litres beef stock
1 large floury potato
600g bunch of beetroot
200g good quality stewing steak
Salt and pepper
2 tablespoon red wine vinegar
Smidge of sugar
200ml sour cream / crème fraiche
Dill, washed and chopped into small fronds

<u>Method</u>

In a large saucepan, start by putting it on a medium heat, with a dash of sunflower oil and the butter. Add the three base vegetables, onion, celery, and carrot, all diced into small pieces. Cook them with the pan lid on, moving them around a bit, for a few minutes until the onion is going translucent.

Then add the crushed garlic, and cook slightly, before pouring in the beef stock. Add the bay leaf and heat to a simmer.

Peel the potato and cut into 1cm dice, and add to the saucepan.

THE ABLE DIABETIC

Meanwhile, wearing rubber gloves if you want to avoid major staining to your hands, peel top and tail the beetroots, discarding the dirty bits, and then wash thoroughly. Dice ¾ of them, and grate the last ¼. The dice should be about 1cm cubes. Beetroot can be quite a muddy veg so make sure you've got clean dice if necessary rinsing again, and then put in the pot.

Simmer this for about 40 minutes, and then test the beetroot to see if the cubes are tender and soft. If they are, use a hand blender to pulse the soup into a regular consistency. Keep on a gentle heat.

At this point, add the stewing steak which needs to have been cut into very small pieces suitable for a soup, and the grated beetroot. Cook for a further 15m.

Before serving, add the salt and pepper, the vinegar and the sugar. Taste and adjust with any of those seasonings if you wish.

The soup is ready to serve. Ladle it into deep soup bowls, and swirl sour cream on the top, then scatter a good amount of chopped dill over the top. It's aromatic, fresh, luxurious, and sustaining all in one bowl.

LIFE FOOD

Smoked haddock and sweetcorn chowder

I think of chowder as being a New England thing through and through, and since my year living there fills me with affection every time I think of it, maybe that's why this recipe needs inclusion, despite substituting the clams which are standard in that part of the world, for haddock. More likely, it's because irrespective of its roots, it's a special kind of soup, in the treat category.

Chowder is more of a meal than many soups, containing fish, veg, potato and cream. It can be made lighter still than my recipe if you prefer by omitting the cream and reducing the potato to half the quantity, and will still taste delicious. I have made a key change though. Cauliflower is an unusual ingredient in chowder, but is added here because it is white, its flavour pairs well with cream and fish, and it helps make the chowder much lower carb than it would otherwise be.

It is nice to eat chowder with a nice piece of crusty white bread and butter alongside, and this lower carb version should allow you to do that and not overdo the carbs overall.

Ingredients

Glug of sunflower oil
1 onion, chopped finely
1 small-medium cauliflower, finely chopped up
1 tablespoon plain flour
1 large floury potato
150g piece smoked haddock
300g can sweetcorn
Smidge cayenne pepper
Smidge cumin
Salt & white pepper
150ml single cream
Parsley, chopped finely

THE ABLE DIABETIC

<u>Method</u>

Start with a large saucepan on the hob, with the small amount of sunflower oil, and warm over a medium heat. Add to this the onion, and sweat with the lid on for a few minutes, then tip in the chopped cauliflower.

Peel, wash and dice the potato. The dice should be under 1cm big, because you want them to cook and somewhat disintegrate into the soup. Add the diced potato, then the flour, and mix it in well with the other ingredients. Then pour over 1.5 litres of water and bring to a simmer. Cook for about 15 minutes until the potato and cauliflower are fully cooked through.

Cut the smoked haddock into smallish pieces and add to the pan with the drained tin of sweetcorn. Cook for another 3 minutes by which time the fish will be cooked, and then add the cayenne, cumin, salt and white pepper. Pour over the single cream.

Serve the soup with the fresh parsley sprinkled on top.

Pho

Jim and I travelled in Vietnam for about a month soon after we met, and Pho is considered the national breakfast dish. We ate a lot of it, in some truly basic cafés, and it was always, always, always amazingly good. Vietnam is a hot place, incredibly humid, and it's pretty stunning that a superhot broth-soup would be such a mainstay. But it works.

The stock quality matters for pho. There isn't a lot to this soup, and so the flavour in the base broth dictates the quality of the meal. In Vietnam, the broth is almost always beef. It will have been made with bones simmered for a good while. If you want to do this, butchers will give you bones for not much cost at all. I am conscious that there is some energy involved in simmering bones for hours, but when I do it I make enough stock to freeze that will cover another 6 meals. You can use chicken if you prefer, or vegetable stock. In both cases the ultimate soup will be different but still good. Try to make sure the stock is good and flavourful.

A key thing over there is that the coriander and mint used in the soup is incredibly abundant and cheap. It's not like that in the UK where you pick up a few stems in the supermarket (in plastic, give me strength!) and its pretty pricey. Ideally, this soup should have loads of herbs thrown in just before you eat it. And superhot chillis, sliced up finely.

Serves 4

Ingredients

1.5 litres stock – ideally beef bone broth, but you can use chicken or vegetable
300g rice noodles
200g beef steak
Fresh bean sprouts
Large bunch of fresh coriander

THE ABLE DIABETIC

Large bunch of mint
Red and green birds' eye / hot chillies
Half a bunch of spring onions
4 limes
Fish sauce
Soy sauce

<u>Method</u>

Although I suppose this is cooking, it is so quick, and much more of an assembly exercise than cooking. Do the prep before you start.

Make sure your beef is well chilled or even semi frozen, trim of all fat and sinew, and cut it (raw) into very thin slices, then set aside.

Wash the bean sprouts.

The herbs make this meal. Wash the coriander and mint. Take all the leaves off the coriander and cut the stalks into tiny pieces. Roughly cut the leaves. With the mint, remove the leaves from stems, and discard the stems. Lightly chop the leaves. Get the prepared herbs into one big pile ready to serve.

Chop the chillis into tiny dice. Put in a serving dish.

Wash the spring onions and discard root and top of the green, and slice the rest up.

Quarter the limes.

To make the pho, get a large 2 litre saucepan and fill with the stock. Heat this up to boiling and let it bubble for a few minutes (this is mainly for food safety). This is pretty much all you have to do, so be ready to serve quickly.

The penultimate stage is to season. Add the soy sauce and the fish sauce, a dash of each, and taste the pho to check it is tasty. You may need to add more of either, depending on if it is tangy from the fish sauce and salty from the soy. It is better to leave it so people can add more individually than overdo it though!

Into the boiling stock put the rice noodles, and give them 2 minutes simmering. Take the pot off the heat. Serve the pho into large bowls, and immediately add the steak to the bowls, then the bean sprouts. The heat of the pho will cook both.

The pho is ready to eat, and everyone should add the herbs, chillis, lime juice and more fish and soy sauces as they wish.

Nothing quite like it!

MAINS

MAINS

Lentil and mushroom Bolognese

Roast chicken and green salad

Pea, lemon and chicken risotto

Vegetable crumble

Mexican eggs

Dhal plus plus

Pakoras

Roast jeera cauliflower and carrots

Pesto cod, mash and green vegetables

Ratatouille

Homity pie

Moroccan aubergine couscous

Sweet potato enchiladas

Salmon and broccoli filo quiche

Gish's lentil quiche

Rainbow noodles

Spinach and brown rice bake

Mackerel and tomato pasta

Lauren's cayenne chicken farfalle

Sausage and borlotti bean casserole

Bean burgers and sweet potato fries

Spicy Ricey

Kedgeree

Carpenter's pie

Halloumi kebabs and brown rice

Green mac 'n' cheese

Lamb and lentil moussaka

Sweet potato and filo parcels

Puy lentil, feta and red pepper pie

Beef and black bean noodles

Roast aubergine, chickpea mash and harissa

Seared tuna, cannellini bean mash, roast tomatoes and olives

LIFE FOOD

General guidance on eating for type 1 diabetics says that it is best to stick to eating at mealtimes, and not snacking or grazing, because that means your high glucose period post meals will only occur at limited times, and also that the amount of carbohydrate you eat should always be controlled and not too large. I agree that this is a good approach.

A main meal, by definition, is when you eat a larger meal, and so while it needs to be sustaining, it also needs to be carefully put together. My approach to what I eat for my main meal has been shaped by years of work on getting this element right.

There are some significant challenges for me with the evening meal being my main meal. The first is size. It is the largest meal of the day. By the time I get to it I am usually pretty hungry which carries the risk of over-eating. I've been overweight for most of my adult life, not because I eat bad food, but because I am not great with portion control, and this is especially the case when I'm ravenous after a long day at work.

I was brought up eating a lot of carbs at mealtimes, and that carried into my adult habits, and has taken a long time to moderate. Eating a lot of carbs at any time means a large blood glucose peak, which is hard for insulin to keep up with. Eating a carb-laden meal in the evening creates the challenge that it'll take 2 to 3 hours, to digest, and that means that I can still have the impact on my blood sugar happening after I go to bed, leading to unpredictable highs and lows of blood glucose through the night. In my life this has often been exacerbated by the meal being eaten late. With the best will in the world, in my working life I have frequently found myself eating after 7.30pm in the evening, sometimes substantially later, and that is, in truth, too late to be healthy.

What this means is that I have to ensure that what I do eat in my main meal doesn't contain too much carbohydrate. Some, but not too much. Enough that I don't want to eat a few biscuits before bed. This is real life, and I have the same challenges as a non-type 1 diabetic in needing willpower to stop me from grabbing a snack. From the outside maybe the fact that it is essential to manage carbs seems to convey that us t1ds are granted some miraculous ability to not be tempted by the biscuit tin. I can say clearly and unreservedly that is not the case. So, making sure meals are satiating as well as controlled is the objective.

Getting back to evening time eating, although I've long been aware of the challenges of eating my main meal in the evening, my life doesn't readily accommodate anything different, so I accept it and work with it as best as I can. Being prepared as much as possible so that dinner can be ready as early as possible after I finish work is helpful. This translates into some meals which are super-quick to prep, but mainly into making food at the weekend in readiness for the week ahead. That way it doesn't have to be me who puts it in the oven either. A lot of my cooking is capable of being prepped ahead and warmed up when needed.

The prepping ahead also has the benefit that what I eat is made when I have time and can make it well. As with all my food, there are a lot of vegetables and pulses in my meals. There is some work in putting it together. It's worth it because it's much better to come home to a veggie chilli that just needs warming up, than find myself making a plate of spaghetti with a jar of shop-bought sauce.

A lot of my meals swap out carbs, and meat, that would be in the 'classic version' for alternatives which make the overall meal better for me. Reducing the carb-load but keeping things substantial and satisfying is how I try to adjust things.

Portion size is a big challenge for me. I'm rather inclined to have "just a little bit more". I therefore find portioning up as part of the prep process can be quite beneficial by getting rid of the option of seconds. As a result, I like making food in individual portions.

I think we eat well as a family. There's a lot of variety, a lot of vegetables, not a lot of waste, careful use of meat, and generally

LIFE FOOD

happy stomachs. These recipes incorporate the experience of many years of practice and tweaks.

THE ABLE DIABETIC

Lentil and mushroom Bolognese

I remember spaghetti Bolognese being my favourite when I was about 8, and it holds true in our household that it's right up there as a cornerstone favourite.

We still eat a classic meat-based Bolognese quite often, although it is common for me to add green or puy-style lentils to the Bolognese sauce.

In this recipe, I go fully veg-focused, mainly driven by health objectives, and I think this is a flavourful sauce for pasta. The longer it can be simmered the better it will be, and like many other things, it will increase the depth of flavour if left in the fridge for a couple of days. If you do this, you will likely have to slightly loosen it with a dash of water because anything lentilly will keep on absorbing moisture, but that's it.

From my perspective as a t1d, it is important that when I eat pasta there is a balance between the amount of pasta and whatever gets put on it. I know that Italians eat pasta simply, with only a touch of sauce dressing the pasta, and the pasta itself is the main thing, but in my world, that's a dangerous way to go and leads to too much carb, which hits blood sugars hard. My body works best when there's quite a lot of veg in the mix, so by design, the portion of sauce is relatively large.

To be honest, I can't see Italians objecting much.

Serves 4

Ingredients

1 large brown onion, diced small
3 sticks celery, diced small
2 large carrots, diced small
4 fat cloves garlic

THE ABLE DIABETIC

Sunflower oil
Olive oil
150g dry Puy-style lentils, rinsed in a sieve
300g of chestnut mushrooms, cleaned and sliced
Tinned tomatoes – 1-2 tins – 400g each
Salt and pepper

300g Spaghetti, or other pasta, cooked as per instructions

Parmesan, pecorino, or cheddar to serve

<u>Method</u>

In a medium saucepan, heat a glug of sunflower oil, and add the onion, celery, carrot mixture. Sauté over a medium heat for a few minutes until starting to look translucent, but not brown. Add the crushed garlic and the mushrooms, and continue to cook over the meat for a few minutes so that the mushrooms have started to give up some of their liquid content.

Add the tinned tomatoes and the puy lentils. This mixture needs to simmer on the hob for at least 40 minutes and likely longer (longer is better), which I would do with the lid on. You may need to add some additional water too, as the lentils will absorb liquid as they cook.

After 40 minutes, the Bolognese will be cooked enough to serve, so it is time to taste and season with the salt and pepper, and to add the olive oil, again to enhance the taste and texture.

At this final stage, put on a pan of water for the pasta, and bring to the boil. Cook the pasta as appropriate for the variety of pasta. I like to serve this with spaghetti or linguine, but penne would do just as well. This is not precious cooking.

Serve with the option of grated hard cheese on the side. I must admit this is considered essential by every member of my family.

LIFE FOOD

Roast chicken and green salad

Roast chicken is a gift of a meal. I love the wintry version with roast potatoes, a range of vegetable sides, stuffing and gravy. I also find alternatives shaped by inspiration from all manner of other cuisines are a great way to ring the changes. Smothering your chicken in tandoori spice and baking with rice added to the juices towards the end is fabulous, as is doing what one of my MOB cookbooks suggests and going peri-peri seasoning in the style of Nando's. This is genius in my book as you can have the fun of the take-out style with the ethics of your own good quality chicken.

Quality matters. In my cooking, care for the animal, and an ethos of waste reduction drive one of the key reasons for cooking a roast chicken which is that there is always an opportunity for some kind of leftovers meal, even if it just stock, and pretty much the whole bird gets used.

Of all the ways to east roast chicken, one way gives me joy above all others. A summer day and a roast chicken and green salad with a punchy, Dijon-y, dressing is my idea of perfection. There is something about new potatoes, lovely leaves, and chicken that makes a perfect mouthful.

This is also a nicely balanced meal, simple, but good for a t1d, combining as it does a good amount of leaves, and some readily measurable carbs in the form of the potatoes.

The relaxed nature of the meal also translates into the rhythm of its preparation. There is no need for the chicken or potatoes to be served hot, so make the salad and the dressing at some point while the chicken roasts, and cook the potatoes so they are ready before the chicken is. I think it's lovely when both chicken and potatoes are still somewhat warm, but not too much.

Serves 4

THE ABLE DIABETIC

<u>Ingredients</u>
Medium – large fresh chicken, about 1.5kg
1 lemon
Bunch of tarragon
50g butter / good dollop of sunflower oil

New potatoes 800g
30g butter

Lettuce leaves: ideally soft, green, varieties such as English round, lambs' lettuce, butterhead, little gem

Olive oil
White wine vinegar
Dijon mustard
Salt & pepper

<u>Method</u>

Put the chicken free of all its wrapping in a suitable roasting dish and stuff the lemon and tarragon into the chicken's cavity. Spread butter or sunflower oil over the breast of the chicken. Put this into an oven preheated to 160 C. Roast for the time advised on the packaging, which will be about 1 hour 20 minutes, and check it is cooked by inserting a skewer or similar tool into the deepest part of its thigh to check that the juices run clear.

Remove from the oven, cover in foil, and leave to rest for 20 minutes at least.

Meanwhile, you have the chicken cooking time to do the rest of the prep.

Prepare the salad by washing the leaves and putting them in a bowl. Make the salad dressing by whisking together the oil, vinegar and Dijon, and salt & pepper.

Cook the new potatoes in a saucepan of boiling water, simmering for about 30m or until the potatoes are tender when a knife is put into them. Drain, and transfer to a serving bowl.

When the chicken has rested and you're ready to serve, transfer the chicken to a suitable platter. Either dress the leaves and toss or leave the dressing for others to add.

Definitely best served outside on a sunny day.

# THE ABLE DIABETIC

Pea, lemon and chicken risotto

I am religious about the way I cook chicken. A couple of decades ago when people seemed to eat nothing but chicken breasts, I started to go out of my way to buy thighs and drumsticks, and developed my cooking around using them. Eventually, I have graduated to a position where I almost never buy anything other than a whole chicken, and I make typically, at least 3 meals from it. The first is a classic roast. The second, something like a curry, and the third is stock based, like this risotto.

I have a lot of time for vegetarians and vegans. I know it sounds harsh, but I don't have a lot of time for people who eat with no consideration for the planet, other beings, or just the effects of their choices. I have spent my life eating meat, and I value and enjoy it, but I recognise that my choices matter. As a family, we've always eaten less meat and more vegetables, and that is a principle that has an increasing impact over time.

I feel that if I am going to eat meat, then I need to choose carefully and put some effort into maximising its value.

So, once we've had our roast dinner, I strip the whole carcass down, and sort the meat. The chunky stuff, breast, thighs especially, goes into the pile that forms the basis of meal #2. There's another pile which is for the bitty stuff: from the wings, and towards the end of the stripping down process. The surprising thing, for those of you who haven't done this, is how much meat you end up with. More than enough in this 'bitty pile' for a risotto.

The bones, skin, everything goes in a stock pot. Personally, I don't add onion, carrots etc at this stage, it's just water and the carcass. Covered with water this is simmered at a low heat for a long time. Hours. Lid is on. I try to get as much of the cartilage around the joints into the stock. All of that is good, nutritional stuff.

LIFE FOOD

I'm including risotto in this collection even though as a t1d you do have to be careful with portion control. It is easy to make more, or eat a larger portion than you should, and at the end of the day, a risotto is rice is carbs. However, it is also satisfying and healthy. I like to do what Italians do and have something before the risotto itself, for example a small salad. Their way of little courses, a starter, then some pasta / rice, then some meat, is a good way of enjoying food, and creating balance.

Serves 4

Ingredients

1 white onion, chopped finely
A knob of butter and a splash of sunflower oil
Splash vermouth or dry white wine
300g risotto rice (arborio or carnaroli)
Chicken stock 300-400ml, hot (and sieved so it is clear)
The chicken scraps from the carcass (doesn't matter how much but as a guide about 200g)
300g frozen peas
1 lemon, juiced
If you want… you can add a dollop of cream, single, double, crème fraiche, doesn't matter.

Method

Before you start – get in the right mood. The creaminess of a risotto comes from the stirring of it as it gently cooks. It is said that creamy risotto is because of the love it is made with, through the stirring which disperses the rice's starch. So, give yourself time, and enjoy the action of standing near the pan, stirring often, and putting your love into the dish.

You'll need a large wide pan, suitable for taking the volume of rice once it has grown through the absorption of the stock.

THE ABLE DIABETIC

Put the pan on the heat, to a medium level, and add the knob of butter, sunflower oil, and once the butter has melted, the chopped onion. Be careful about the heat as you cook the onion because you don't want browning, but just for the onion to go translucent.

Once it has, add the rice and stir to coat with the buttery onions, then add the splash of vermouth or wine. By the way, the risotto will still be delicious if you decide you don't want alcohol. Stir for a few moments, and then start to add the hot stock ladle by ladle. Stir the risotto every few moments, making sure that nothing catches on the bottom of the pan, and it is bubbling gently but not aggressively. My rhythm is to stir, go and do a little job like getting the bowls out, or prepping the salad, and then to come back and stir again: an on / off rhythm all the way. The whole process is gentle and soothing. Whenever the rice seems to be getting a bit sticky, add some more stock.

The chicken pieces, which will be cold, do need to be added in time for them to get fully hot, for food safety reasons, so I stir them in about halfway through cooking the rice i.e. 10 minutes in. It depends slightly on how large they are because they get affected by the stirring action too. Make sure they have had several minutes at full heat.

After about 25m total cooking time, the rice will be close to ready. Making risotto is an art not a science so the thing to do is to take a grain and bite it with your front teeth to see if there is any uncooked texture in the middle. Once you can bite through with no resistance, you're close to the end.

Add the frozen peas and the lemon juice at this point, and keep stirring until the peas are cooked. Timing is a thing here because in order to keep the peas bright green you don't want to overcook the whole thing, but you need to factor in a bit of resting.

Once the peas are unfrozen and slightly cooked, turn the heat off, and let the pan stand for 2-5 minutes. You'll see that the risotto continues to get creamier and just a touch less runny, which makes for a better texture. This is also the point when you would add cream if you wished. Nigel Slater once described this as gilding the lily, and he's right: not necessary at all, but adds something extra.

Serve the risotto on wide soup plates and let everyone feel the love!

The finished risotto benefits from salt and white pepper, so let people do that themselves.

Vegetable crumble

So, no new news in that I love vegetables. What I love about a vegetable crumble is that you can make it new every time and vary it according to what is available. The secret to this being in a winner in my view is having a gentle and slightly creamy vegetable bottom layer with a crunchy, savoury, textural top layer.

Also, no news, is that as well as eating enough veg, we should all be eating a wide variety of different types of fruit, veg, nuts and seeds. I am a little odd in that I like to count how many I've managed recently (and also smug because it is usually a lot). A meal like this offers so much opportunity to max out on variety. You can use several veg in the underlayer, and add nuts, seeds, grains to the top layer. The only thing that matters when you come to varying things is that in the preparation stage the veg are all cooked to a point where they are a touch underdone (as they will finish cooking in the last stage).

This dish is an effective and appealing way of making the ratio of carb-based topping just enough for the t1d eating it. It's not like a shepherd's pie with a vast pillow of mash on top which I always have to treat with care! Despite the topping being a thinnish layer, it is savoury and still satisfying.

This is pretty close to be an ideal version for me...

Serves 4

Ingredients

Glug of sunflower oil
2 sticks celery, sliced into small pieces
3 large carrots, peeled and diced to 1cm
2 leeks – with the top and the root sliced off and then cut into rounds (wash well of course)
300g button / white / chestnut mushrooms, wiped and sliced

LIFE FOOD

2 medium parsnips, peeled and diced a little larger than the carrots
2 medium sweet potato, peeled and diced like the parsnip
sage, thyme, and rosemary, finely chopped

Sauce:
75g butter,
75g plain flour,
750ml milk,
Salt & white pepper
100g cheddar, ideally mature, grated

Topping:
175g wholemeal flour,
120g lard / butter, cubed
75g oats,
75g cheddar, grated
75g chopped hazelnuts
50g sunflower seeds (or other seeds)

Method

You'll need an ovenproof dish about 30cm x 20cm.

In a large saucepan, warm a good glug of sunflower oil and put the chopped celery and carrot in and stir to coat with the oil. Put the lid of the pan on, and let cook for a minute or two. Don't let anything catch on the bottom. Then add the leeks, chopped parsnips, and chopped sweet potato, and stir everything up again. The objective of this part of the process is to cook all the veg until it is on the point of tender, and if you put a knife into a piece of vegetable it retains some resistance. So put a small dash of water into the pan and the lid on and let the steam help with the cooking. You want to add the mushrooms about 3 minutes before all the other veg are at the 'just cooked' point. Having said all that, nothing disastrous is going to happen if things are overcooked! Try not to burn anything though. Once the veg is cooked, take off the heat, sprinkle on the herbs, leave to cool slightly.

THE ABLE DIABETIC

In a separate and smaller saucepan, make the sauce. Melt the butter until liquid, stir in the flour, and combine to get the roux, the smoother paste, then add a little milk and stir. Gradually add the milk, whisking it as you go, so that the sauce is not lumpy, all the while heating the sauce. You have to cook the sauce once all the milk is added so that it goes fully thick. This will take a few minutes. As it's cooking, it will try to stick to the bottom and corners of the pan, so make sure that you are whisking / mixing it to avoid this. Once the sauce is finished, thick and ready, take it off the heat and stir in the grated cheddar and the salt and pepper. Put aside to cool.

Lastly, make the crumble topping. You can either do this in a food processor or by hand. It says something about my laziness that I am usually too busy to take the food processor out, unbox it, use and wash it up, so I do it by hand. Yes, I know, crazy. If you do it in the food processor, put in the flour, the lard or butter, and pulse until the mixture resembles fine breadcrumbs. Then stir in all the other ingredients until well mixed. If you do this by hand, in a largish bowl, put the flour and lard / butter, and firstly cut the fat into the flour, then rub the fat into the flour using just your fingertips. This is an easy thing to do. As you're doing it, shake the bowl a bit and the yet to be rubbed lumps will come to the top where you can rub them in. Once you have breadcrumb style crumble, stir in the oats, cheddar and nuts and seeds.

The next step in assembling everything. Put the veg in your ovenproof dish, pour over the cheese sauce, and spoon the crumble on top evenly distributing it. Do this in your own style: it can be smoothed and pristine or lumpy and bumpy. Both will be delicious, and both will look great.

When you want to eat this, bake it in the oven. If immediately, while all the component elements are warm, it'll only take 20 minutes in a 180 degree oven. But if you've chilled it and taken it from the fridge, you'll need about 35 minutes. The top should be crispy and caramel brown when you serve it.

LIFE FOOD

I know it seems a bit mad to add even more veg, but serving a combination of steamed broccoli, peas, and savoy cabbage, onto which you've squeezed some lemon juice pre-serving, is a wonderful way to balance the richness of the crumble.

THE ABLE DIABETIC

Mexican eggs

In all honesty, I don't love eggs. I eat them, but a bit fussily. For me, they need to be well-cooked and ideally, well-disguised. I can't abide a soft boiled egg, nor a poached one where the white is a bit undercooked. It's a food regret because I know how nutritious they are, and from an ethical standpoint, a happy chicken seems a much better place to get your animal protein from than pretty much anything else. We only buy eggs that are from chickens that get freedom and to live like chickens are meant to. Eggs are a cheap food, and I'd rather pay that little bit more than splurge on any number of other food-related nice-to-haves.

Soapbox moment over, this is a fabulous recipe, ultra satisfying and vibrant, and healthy too.

To an extent this is an assembly meal. You prep the various elements in parallel then join them up on the plate at the end.

The va-va-voom comes from the abundant garlic, chilli, coriander and lime juice. Don't be shy when you're cooking this one!

The t1d assessment is that this is recommended too. One slice of wholemeal bread, plus the carbs in the black beans, means enough but not too many carbs, and the multitude of vegetable and protein you get from the other ingredients, makes this a wonderful meal for me.

Makes a great brunch, lunch or supper dish.

Serves 4

Ingredients
=======

Tin black beans (400g) drained and rinsed
3 cloves garlic
Pinch chilli flakes

LIFE FOOD

Glug sunflower oil
3 tomatoes
1 red onion
Red chilli
Fresh coriander

1 large avocado
1 lime, juiced

4 slices wholemeal, seedy bread (ideally cut from a loaf)

4-8 eggs (depending on hunger levels)

1 lime to serve

Method

Start by making the bean mixture, which is essentially Mexican refried beans, except that I recommend minimising the frying bit. In a small saucepan, put a glug of sunflower oil, and heat gently, then add the black beans, the chilli flakes, and the crushed garlic, and mash into a fairly smooth pulp. If it's hard to work, add some water. You're after a bean mash. Get it to hot, and keep this warm as you prep the other items.

Make a tomato salsa but chopping the tomatoes finely, then the red onion finely too, and the red chilli which is finely chopped, and combine in a bowl. Wash the coriander and reserve some, and then finely shop the stalks, reserving the pretty leaves. Mix the chopped stalks into the salsa. Put to one side.

Then make the avocado smash by removing the avocado flesh, and mashing in a bowl with the lime juice and some of the reserved coriander, again chopping up the stalks and reserving the leaves. Put to one side.

THE ABLE DIABETIC

You are now ready for the final stage which you need to do immediately before serving.

Get the bread ready to toast. Toast it as the eggs are cooking, and just before serving.

Finally, fry your eggs. If you are doing 8, you'll need to be organised. I heat the top oven up slightly, and put a baking tray in to warm before starting to fry the eggs, so the first 4 can sit in there while I fry the last 4. However you do it, you want a set of 8 fried eggs ready to serve.

The assembly of the final plates involves toast first, onto which you put the black bean mixture, then the avocado smash, then the tomato salsa. On top of that, place the fried eggs, 1 or 2 per plate, and scatter over the reserved coriander leaves.

Serve with a wedge of lime per plate, plus salt, and extra chilli either flakes or chopped fresh. Part of the fun of this meal is dialling up the zing to your personal taste. In our house it verges into a fun competition!

LIFE FOOD

Dhal plus plus

The bulk red lentils of uni life led beyond soup, and to dhal. Sadly, my first few efforts were Not A Success. My memory has tried to block that out, but I know that I ended up with something more akin to baby food than anything that could be adult sustenance. On the Indian subcontinent dhal is a daily foodstuff so I knew I was doing something wrong! In time, I worked out how to improve mainly by eating dhal in restaurants; it's helpful to know what you're aiming for.

These days, dhal is one of my favourite meals, and we eat it frequently at home. I do think that just dhal or dhal + rice can be a bit lacking in terms of texture and variety. Also, it's pretty carb heavy. So, the plus plus is because I like to add other things into the mix and there are several things that I go for. I suggest adding two side orders, maybe three, depending on your time, stamina and ambition levels. Some of our favourites are:

Easy pakoras – recipe follows
Roast jeera cauliflower and/or carrots – recipe follows
Kachumber salad – a mix of raw cucumber, tomato & onion chopped salad
Raita – yogurt with cucumber and mint mixed through it
Aubergines, roasted with oil, lots of chopped garlic and chilli
Spinach, stir fried with garlic

All of these things are low carb, but bring zing, and extra dimensions to your plate.

The last thing I'll say is that while we embrace the vegetarian-ness of this in general, Greg in his teen years has wanted meat more. Adding a few grilled chicken thighs to this meal rather than vegetable sides is super easy and means that the meal is a great way of satisfying enthusiastic meat-eaters and veggies side by side. So that works.

THE ABLE DIABETIC

As for this dhal, well it is mine. There are a lot of different approaches to dhal. One of the most thoughtful and imaginative presents I've ever been given was a basket with an array of different sorts of pulses and spices and "The Dal Cookbook". (Thank you, lovely Amrita!) I enjoyed experimenting a lot. I am a particular fan of black dhal, but on an everyday basis I make this one which is based on a combination of red lentils (masoor dhal) and yellow split peas (chana dhal).

My last comment here – a small spoonful of the pear chutney, recipe at the end of this book, goes brilliantly well with this meal too!

Serves 4-8 (depending on sides)

Ingredients

200g red lentils
2 teaspoon turmeric
1 teaspoon chilli flakes
½ teaspoon salt
Boiling water to cover
2 teaspoon tomato puree
4-6 cloves garlic, minced

2 large onions, sliced
Sunflower oil (about 70ml)
40g butter
2 teaspoon jeera (cumin seeds)
4 cloves garlic, crushed

Method

Start by putting the red lentils in a saucepan with enough room for them to double their size, and add the turmeric, the salt and the chilli flakes. Pour over the boiling water to 1cm over the lentils, add the tomato puree and the crushed garlic and stir. Heat the saucepan on the hob, on a medium heat, so that it is just simmering, for about 25 minutes. Check them as they cook in case you need to add more water. When cooked, the lentils will just be a mush, and you may have to stir to stop the bottom from sticking in the last stages.

Separately, in a frying pan, heat a generous glug of sunflower oil over a medium to high heat, and add the onions. Fry them actively for 5-10 minutes until they are all golden brown. Add the jeera and the crushed garlic and cook for a further 2 minutes, then take the pan off the heat and add the butter. Once it has melted, pour the whole lot over the cooked lentils and mix through. This last stage completely changes the dish adding great mouth feel and flavour.

Serve alongside rice and whatever other dishes you've chosen.

THE ABLE DIABETIC

Pakoras

I don't deep fry food so I would never have made my own pakoras unless I had come across an article in The Guardian, part of an anti-food waste series, that said (I'm paraphrasing) "this is a brilliant way to use peelings from veg to make food people will eat". I thought "why not?", and adopted it as something that had utility. It also made clear that it was totally something you could make your own. Which is how I like it.

If I recall rightly, the cooking method was still deep fried, and so I have adapted: I shallow fry but with liberal quantities of oil.

Whether you use the actual peelings from veg is up to you. I don't raid the compost bin. But I do use the whole veg whatever I put in these.

A top tip I have is about the size you make these. Usually, we have them alongside dhal or as part of a curry meal, as a side, and so I make them about 5cm diameter. I've also made them as 'party nibbles' in much smaller morsels that are essentially a straightforward mouthful. And, last but not least, I've made them burger sized, and they work amazingly well in burger buns with chips on the side, although this is a heavy dose of carbs, so not honestly one for me.

The amount of carbs they contain depends on what veg they're made of, how big they are, and how many you eat. They are not carb free. So, tread with care. But the gram (chickpea) flour they are made of is roughly half the carbs compared to wheat flour weight for weight, and when made with onions, carrots, and green leaves (cabbage, cauliflower leaves, spinach, etc) which are my standards, they aren't too impactful.

The last thing to say is that in the spirit of massive flexibility, I am rather random with the spices used in this. If there are jars that are in the Indian suite and I need to use them up, in they go! Adds to the fun. I especially like adding seeds, nigella, mustard, cumin, fennel etc.

This recipe is the essence of frugal and easy going.

Serves: this amount makes about the right amount for sides to one meal for the 4 of us.

Ingredients:

100g gram flour (made from chickpeas)
1 teaspoon salt
1 teaspoon cumin seeds
1 teaspoon nigella
1 teaspoon chilli flakes
½ teaspoon turmeric

300g of clean vegetable peelings / gratings / small pieces (I use carrots, onions, spring onions, leaves of any kind, chopped up cauliflower (especially the middle part), courgettes, celery leaves, sweet potato, butternut squash, parsnip, sometimes potato)

Oil for frying (sunflower)
Some fresh coriander, chutneys, and yogurt to serve

Method

Make the batter ahead of time. It needs to stand for at least 30 minutes and preferably longer. Since it takes approximately 2 minutes to make it, this isn't a difficult thing to get ahead of.
Put the gram flour, salt, spices in a bowl that will be large enough to accommodate the veg later, and whisk together with 150ml of cold water. The consistency of the batter should be that of double cream, so somewhat spoonable but runny. It will slightly thicken after being left.

THE ABLE DIABETIC

When you are ready to make the pakoras, prep the veg, and put all the gratings into the batter and mix well to combine.

In a large wide frying pan, heat the sunflower oil to a high heat. When I say this needs a generous amount, I am talking a few millimetres, not a centimetre. You do have to top it up as you're going though because the pakoras absorb a fair bit. Add spoonfuls of the vegetable batter to the pan and fry for about 3 minutes. Try not to move the pakoras until they are ready to flip. You may need to adjust the heat a bit to ensure that the middles are getting cooked as well as the outside browned and crispy. Flip when ready and cook for another 3 minutes on the other side. Keep warm in a slightly warm oven if needed, until you eat.

These pakora warm up remarkably well if they don't get eaten immediately. Leftovers in our house often become a lunchtime hot sarnie for the boys.

LIFE FOOD

Roast jeera cauliflower and carrots

While I'm including this because it goes well alongside the dhal as described above, I think this is a spectacular meal in itself, and happily eat it as a meal with some rice or naan bread on the side.

Serves 4-6

Ingredients

1 cauliflower
4 medium carrots
Sunflower or rapeseed oil
3 cloves crushed garlic
3teaspoon ground cumin
3 teaspoon cumin seeds (jeera)
A pinch salt

Method

This can be made on a baking tray or in an ovenproof dish (which you can take straight to the table).

Pre-heat the oven to 180° C / 350° F / Gas mark 4.

Wash the cauliflower well, including the leaves. Cut the bottom off the cauliflower, and then cut a deep cross in the bottom of it, and break the cauliflower apart, trying to keep the leaves attached to the base florets. I like to use the leaves, both for their look, and to prevent food waste, and they survive cooking best if still attached. Once you have separated all the florets, ideally into similar sizes, put them in a largish bowl.

Prepare the carrots by peeling, topping, tailing, and then cutting into large chunks – about 2cm long. Put them into the bowl too.

THE ABLE DIABETIC

Mix together the oil, crushed garlic, salt, ground cumin and jeera seeds, and pour over the cauliflower and carrots in the bowl. Mix everything around thoroughly. Then put the cauliflower and carrots on the baking sheet or in the ovenproof dish.

Put them in the oven and roast for 35-40 minutes by which time they will be tender, golden and a bit crispy.

Serve immediately.

LIFE FOOD

Pesto cod, mash, and green vegetables

This is a special recipe and the fact that it uses cod means it is one I make sparingly. The many sustainability concerns about white fish have had a big impact on my likelihood of including it in our meals. It's been said that it's crazy that we, as an island nation, don't eat more fish but it doesn't seem odd to me: quite expensive and comes with a huge side order of guilt.

The fish doesn't have to be cod, so use your own judgement in selecting the right white fish for you. A google search tells me current good options for the fish in this recipe are pollock, hake, and cod. Try to get MSC (Marine Stewardship Council) certified fish.

I've included this recipe despite the above concerns because it's super healthy, we should all eat more fish, and it's at the more elegant end of my cooking. Sometimes you want something a bit more elevated.

Originally I made this meal with the mash made from pure potato. Now it's a mixture with cannellini beans in it. This obviously helps the meal in terms of fibre, carb load, and makes for a better glycaemic index number for us t1ds.

Serves 4

Ingredients

4 pieces cod / white fish, 500g total weight
Small amount sunflower oil
200g floury potatoes
400g can cannellini beans, rinsed and drained
50-80ml milk
200g tender stem broccoli
100g peas (frozen)
200g other green veg (green beans, mange tout)
100g green pesto from a jar or tub

50ml extra virgin olive oil
Salt & pepper to serve

<u>Method</u>

There are four elements to this dish – the mash, the veg, the fish and the pesto drizzle. When plating up at the end, they all need to be ready and at the same time, so be a bit careful about timings.

Make the pesto drizzle first. In a small jug mix the pesto with the olive oil until you have a runny pesto sauce. Set aside.

To prepare the mash, peel the potatoes and cut into chunks, then put in a suitable saucepan and boil the potatoes for about 20-30 minutes. 5 minutes from the end of the cooking time, put in the drained cannellini beans to heat through. Then drain everything, and mash thoroughly with the milk. Keep warm.

The vegetables are steamed with all of them in the same pan together. So, cut the broccoli and the green beans/mange tout (or whatever you're using) into sizes that will cook in the same time. Get a pan with 2cm of water to boil as you're cooking the potatoes for the mash, and steam for 5 minutes. Then add the frozen peas and steam for a further 3-4 minutes.

At the same time as you are putting the vegetables on to cook, get a sauté or frying pan that can fit the fish pieces and heat to medium and lightly oil it with the sunflower oil, then place the fish in it and cook for 5-7 minutes, or until cooked. I usually put the lid on so that the fish also lightly steams.

As soon as the fish and vegetables are cooked, plate up, starting with the mash, then the green veg, then the fish. This order just helps it look presentable and pretty. Lastly, drizzle the pesto oil over the fish and mash.

Serve immediately.

LIFE FOOD

Ratatouille

I worked in a wine bar in Truro called Bustopher Jones in my late teens. It was a Truro institution for a long time but sadly it no longer exists. In my day you might have stumbled upon it in the depths of France. It had wooden bistro furniture, a low-lit ambience, and a good wine list. It was jam-packed with eclectic art, and jazz was in its soul. I waitressed and worked Friday and Saturday nights when the place was packed to the gills. Since it was over three floors, the waiting staff ran up and down stairs all the time, laden with earthenware plates and bowls brimming with hearty food.

Bustopher's ratatouille was unlike any ratatouille I have come across anywhere else. It was amazing. Fortunately, it was a staff benefit to get fed. Years later, when the Pixar animated film 'Ratatouille' came out, I found it kind of perfect that they picked ratatouille. It does have profound provenance and soul.

I think my version, which is designed to be as much like the one BJs served as possible, is a pretty good replica. The full version includes the grated cheese on top and the special garlic bread. This is definitely a case of imitation being the highest form of flattery.

I didn't become a t1d until after my Bustopher's years. It turns out that this is a great meal for me, because the main bit is the wonderful vegetable casserole, and although bread comes on the side, being on the side it is entirely manageable! This is definitely a defining recipe of my life.

Serves 4

Ingredients
1 brown onion
4-5 garlic cloves
Abundant extra virgin olive oil
2 aubergines
3 courgettes

THE ABLE DIABETIC

2 400g tins of good quality chopped tomatoes (you may need a third)

Mature cheddar, grated – 200g

Unsliced granary loaf (i.e. malted brown bread with seeds)
Butter
Parsley
Garlic, 3 fat cloves

Method

The ratatouille benefits from a good long simmer, so I recommend that you start this meal a long time before you want to eat it. Alternatively, make it ahead as it will reheat marvellously.

In a large (2 litre) saucepan, heat the olive oil fairly gently, and add the diced onion, then sauté it until it is translucent and just on the point of browning, soft and sweet.

While that's happening, wash and cut up your aubergines. Start by cutting off the stalk and discard. Then cut the aubergines width wise, into slices that are pretty much 2cm thick. Avoid making the aubergine chunks too small as the whole texture of the finished dish will end up a bit lacking. Cut each slice into quarters. Add to the saucepan; you may need to add a bit more olive oil too.

A word about the olive oil. It's well known that aubergines absorb a lot of oil, and they do if you let them. I certainly want some olive oil in my aubergines, but I also make sure to keep it a reasonable amount. You'll find that they don't need as much as they ask for!

Move the aubergines around the pan, and alongside doing that, prep and crush your garlic cloves and add them too. Stir frequently. After a couple more minutes, add the tinned tomatoes. It is hard to predict if you'll need just the 2 tins or 3, because it depends on how big the aubergines were and how they behave – if in doubt err on the side of generosity and put in 3. This is a very tomatoey dish.

LIFE FOOD

Bring that to a simmer, and then maintain at a low simmer for a good long time. I would aim for gentle cooking over 3 hours. You can speed it up, but the character of the dish won't be the same.

There is a lot to be said for slow cooking.

When you're approaching time to serve, get the garlic bread ready. Cut four slices from the granary loaf, making them about 2cm thick (yes! I mean that). Soften the butter in a bowl, and add the garlic (crushed), and the parsley which should be finely chopped, stalks and leaves. Mix all that up well, and slather on the bread. Put the bread on a baking tray, butter side up.

Once the ratatouille is ready heat up the oven (top / small oven only) and bake the bread slices until they are browned and the garlic butter bubbling.

You're ready to serve. Put the ratatouille into largish bowls, with the grated cheddar on top. It will melt happily on its ratatouille pile.

Bon Appetit!

Homity pie

When I was a teenager, living in Cornwall, coming up to London was an exceptionally rare event, and exciting in a way my children will never be able to understand! I don't remember who first took me to Covent Garden, but I thought I'd died and gone to heaven. I loved it. Back then, vegetarian restaurants were rare and the Cranks restaurant and shop, selling entirely veggie food, was a beacon of forward thinking. I loved the Cranks vibe. If I was in Covent Garden I would always buy a brownie from there. The whole experience of being somewhere so metropolitan and buzzy was exciting, and just visiting Cranks was a real treat.

Cranks were known for their Homity Pie, and somewhere along the line, I tried it and loved it. Cranks scaled down a long time ago now, their Homity Pie lost to a few memories like mine I imagine. You sometimes come across Homity pie recipes still, and they are rarely 'pure' and feature lots of extra ingredients, leeks and cheese especially. Undoubtedly delicious, but not how I remember. And in my view, the simpler the better.

One thing I will say is that this 'simple' Homity Pie loves to be accompanied by an array of colourful side salads: leaves (including rocket), coleslaws, beetroot-based, tomato etc. This equates to a veritable feast. It is necessary for me to accompany a moderate slice of Homity pie which is heavily hefty on the carbs with sides which are not! The combination of solid wholemeal pastry and a filling of potato is, well, solid carbs. But my way of managing t1d and food is to make it work, and you can as long as you're thoughtful about what goes alongside the pie.

In terms of side, these are the kind of things I would suggest:
- Leaves / lettuce / spinach
- Slaws, including classic coleslaw, but also spicier Asian-inspired ones with varied cabbage components
- Tomato salad

LIFE FOOD

- Avocado
- Fennel and orange
- Cucumber / tomato / olive
- Roasted courgettes and tomatoes

Serves 8 at least

Ingredients

500g wholemeal flour
250g vegetable shortening (such as Trex)
A pinch of salt

400g floury potatoes
4 garlic cloves (or more if to your taste)
Butter – 50g
Milk – between 50ml-100ml and a spoonful of double cream
Salt & pepper

Method

The first step is to make the pastry. In a bowl with plenty of room, put the flour and pinch of salt in first, then add the vegetable shortening, cut into small cubes. Using the tips of your fingers rub the fat into the flour, making something like breadcrumbs in texture. Try to be light with this, and do it somewhere cold if at all possible. Once you have the breadcrumb texture throughout, add cold water bit by bit and press the mixture together. Don't add too much water because you'll get a sticky, wet mess. You want it to just hold. Squeeze together into a ball, and leave somewhere cold for at least 30m. Pastry isn't hard to make as long as you stick to some basic things: it likes to be cold, handle it as little as you can, and give it the time to rest after making it that allows it to develop its internal bonds.

While the pastry rests, prep the filling. This isn't hard. It is essentially slightly undermashed mash!

THE ABLE DIABETIC

Peel the potatoes, cut into 2 centimetre chunks, and put into a saucepan that has about 4cm of water in it. Bring to a simmer, and cook the potato until tender. Drain the water off.

Because the filling of the pie is so simple, be careful with the mashing stage. You want to just break up the potatoes a bit, so they are crumbly but kind of still in chunks. Before you do the mashing, add the crushed garlic, the butter and the salt and pepper. Doing this before mashing is better than afterwards to make sure they're well distributed without breaking the potato up too much. You will need to add milk and cream too, the amount up to your judgement, and depends on how absorbent the potatoes are.

Once the 'mash' is made, let it cool a bit before assembling the pie.

You can make the pie in any pie dish you fancy. I use a springform cake tin because I like it to stand alone at the end. This recipe is designed to be a proper pie with pastry above and below the filling. So, start by dividing the pastry into 2, in a 60:40 ratio. The bottom of the pie will need more pastry than the top. On a well-floured board, roll out the larger ball of pastry to a wide circle that will fit the tin you are using and carefully press into it. In terms of thickness, for this recipe I err on the side of it being thicker than usual, so about ¾ of a cm rather than the ½ cm I would use if making a quiche. I always find wholemeal pastry a bit harder to handle than white so handle with care. Trim the pastry around the edge. Then spoon the potato mixture into the tin too, and level it off. Roll out the second piece of pastry and place on the top of the pie. Trim to make a neat circle. Use a small amount of milk under the edge, brushed on, to help the bottom and top pieces of pastry connect to each other. Then, using a fork, press the top against the bottom all around the edge to seal. Make a couple of holes in the top of the pie to allow steam to come out during cooking. I do this using scissors, and just snip into the pastry which produces a little v shaped vent.

LIFE FOOD

The pie then needs to go in the oven, at 160° C / 325° F / Gas mark 3, to bake for an hour. It's a solid thing so don't undercook it whatever you do! It'll happily go over time but not under!

When you take it out, let it cool for 10 minutes before taking it out of the tin. This helps to minimise the risk of it collapsing. Alternatively, just serve from the tin! It is possible to take it out and serve standalone as long as you're careful.

THE ABLE DIABETIC

Moroccan aubergine couscous

I'm not sure where this recipe came from. I do know that my appreciation for Moroccan food increased a lot after a trip to Marrakesh with two close friends, Ingrid and Nic. As anyone who has visited knows, Marrakesh is an absolute assault on your senses, with spicy smells, a frenetic but also relaxed energy to it, and rich earthiness everywhere you go.

The food is highly spiced, and contains a lot of fruit alongside meat. The savoury and sweet mingle like the beauty and the roughness of the place.

This recipe doesn't include meat. You don't need it. You get so much flavour and texture from the rest of the ingredients, especially the many spices, and the aubergine provides the richness and substance that meat does in my view.

In keeping with my t1d adjustments, I have included a tin of chickpeas and some red lentils which add to both the body and the suitability of this dish for me as a t1d. Couscous itself has essentially the same nutritional profile as pasta, so far better to have the red lentils and chickpeas on your plate than a big pile of couscous.

Serves 4

Ingredients

Glug of rapeseed or sunflower oil
1 large onion, chopped
4 cloves garlic minced
2 large aubergines
1 400g can chickpeas
½ teaspoon black pepper
½ teaspoon white pepper
1 teaspoon coriander
1 teaspoon cumin

LIFE FOOD

½ teaspoon cinnamon
½ teaspoon ground cloves
½ teaspoon ground nutmeg
1 400g tin chopped tomatoes
100g red lentils, washed
70g dried figs, chopped into pieces (or same weight dates or raisins)
1 large lemon, juice squeezed
200g dried couscous

Method

You need a medium saucepan to make this.

Warm the saucepan on the hob to a medium heat with a good glug of oil (personally I like the colour of rapeseed for this). Add the chopped onion and sauté for a few minutes. While it is cooking, cut the top off the aubergines, and cut into pieces that are mouthful sized, a little under 2cm cubed. Put them in the pan and cook for 8-10 minutes, moving them around, maybe adding a little more oil, as needed.

When the aubergine pieces are starting to go soft, add the garlic and all of the spices, and mix well, allowing the fragrance to develop for 2 minutes.

Then add the tin of tomatoes and stir round well. Add the red lentils, and the rinsed and drained chickpeas. Add the dried figs. Put a little more water in the saucepan so that there is enough liquid that things won't go dry as they cook, about 50-70mls of water.

Keep the pan on a low simmer for an hour, checking the liquid level periodically, and stirring to prevent anything sticking to the base.

Ahead of serving, prepare the couscous according to the packet, which is simple and takes only a few minutes. Pour the lemon juice into the tagine. You are ready to serve.

Sweet potato enchiladas

My son is the enchilada master in our household and since he came home from school having mastered them in a lesson, they've featured frequently. You can put all kinds of things in your tortilla wraps to make enchiladas (although many will be a loooong way from Mexico!). This filling grew to prominence in our family because it ticks the veggie, beany, colourful, and varied boxes.

As I say elsewhere, my son would greatly like to have meat in every meal, but that's not how we roll, so I am looking constantly for ways to make meals that are so tasty he will hardly notice the lack of meat. This chilli recipe succeeds in that.

From my point of view, veggie chillis work well for me. I see them as useful in two ways. As a proper meal, the mainly vegetable core dish doesn't have much in the way of carbs, and so having the enchilada, with 1 tortilla wrap, is a suitable t1d meal. But as I like to minimise carbs a lot through the day, a bowl of the chilli on its own for lunch is perfect. There are carbs – both the beans and the sweet potatoes have some, but the meal overall is low on the glycaemic index, so the carbs are absorbed slowly, and I only need a small dose of insulin to eat the chilli standalone.

The other thing I'll flag here is that this is a brilliant make-ahead feast, which works well in the world of a busy working mum. A tactic I often deploy is making a double quantity of the chilli on a Sunday, using half for enchiladas and the other half for a 'with rice' or 'with tacos' meal, eaten on Monday and Wednesday after work. Seems to work.

Serves 4

Ingredients

Glug of sunflower oil

LIFE FOOD

1 large onion, chopped
2 sticks celery, chopped
4 cloves garlic, crushed
2 teaspoons cumin
1 teaspoon smoked paprika
1 teaspoon chilli powder, or chilli flakes, or chopped fresh chilli
2 large, sweet potatoes
2 tins chopped tomato
1 tin sweetcorn
1 400g tin red kidney beans or black beans
50g dark chocolate
8* tortilla wraps – the large size, about 25cm diameter

100g cheddar, grated

*If I'm making these for my family, I make 2 per person, at least for the boys, but the right level of carbs for me is 1 tortilla, and my daughter tends to have only 1 too. Therefore, you can tailor the recipe by adjusting the number of enchiladas you actually assemble.

Method

Start by getting a medium to large saucepan on the hob, with the glug of sunflower oil in it, warming on a medium heat. Add the chopped onion and celery, put the lid of the saucepan on, and cook for a few minutes, moving the vegetables around so they don't stick or burn, until they are soft and translucent.

Meanwhile, prep the garlic, peeling off the paper skins from the cloves, and the sweet potatoes, which need to be peeled, and then cut into chunky cubes of about 1.5cm. You could go smaller which would be fine, and would cook more quickly, but we prefer that there is texture retained.

Add the crushed garlic, the spices, chilli, and the sweet potato cubes to the saucepan, and stir round for 1-2 minutes. Then add the tins of chopped tomato. Put the lid of the saucepan on, and simmer the chilli for 30 minutes.

After the 30 minutes has elapsed, check how cooked the sweet potato cubes are – there is a bit more cooking to do, but they should be pretty tender when you put a knife into them. If they aren't they need a bit more time. If they are getting there, drain the tin of sweetcorn and put it in the chilli, and then drain and rinse the kidney or black beans and add them too. These don't need cooking, but they do need to be heated through.

The enchiladas work best when the chilli is not too wet, so for the last few minutes of cooking, take the lid off and let steam evaporate away.

Let the chilli cool for at least a few minutes before you prep the enchiladas. I usually prep them well ahead, but you can move faster if needed.

To assemble the enchiladas, you need an ovenproof dish which is big enough for all the enchiladas when rolled up, ideally on one layer, although this is not essential.

Get your tortilla wraps ready, and lay one on a clean worksurface, close to the ovenproof dish. Make each enchilada by putting a large spoonful (about 150ml in volume) on one end of the enchilada and roll up like a Swiss roll, then carefully place in the dish. You can also parcel them up by tucking in first the top and bottom, then roll sideways, which has a different look, but secures the filling a little better. One way of another the objective is to get the wrapped enchilada into the dish with its filling intact! While you're doing this, keep an eye on portion size, and look to save a bit of the chilli for extra. When you have rolled them all, and put them side by side, cuddled up together in the dish, sprinkle the remaining chilli over the top, and then scatter the grated cheddar all over the enchiladas.

The enchiladas need 30 minutes in a hot oven 180in C / 350° F / Gas mark 4. If you have chilled them, i.e. prepped beforehand, give them an extra 5 minutes. They need to be piping hot throughout before you serve.

They can be served as they are. We like to have a green salad with some red onion and tomato on the side. You can also make the meal go further by serving some brown rice alongside, and having everyone get a 1 enchilada portion. It's a brilliantly flexible thing to make.

Salmon and broccoli filo quiche

Quiche is such a boon for all the different guises it can take. It can be solid and hearty, it can be light and elegant. It can contain super fancy ingredients, or be a melange of leftover bits jazzed up into something special. It can be a vegetarian homage or a meaty savoury. So, learning how to make quiche, and how to vary it, is a useful skill to have.

This quiche is a filo one. Two reasons: first, this recipe is a delight; it works well. And second, a filo quiche is a very low carb option that forms a wonderful centre to a balanced meal. I do make quiches with shortcrust pastry, both white and wholemeal, and they have their place. But a slice of that kind of quiche maxes out the carbs that I would have in a meal, and building a meal around that is harder: no potatoes, no croutons, even adding a bean salad for example gets harder. The filo option avoids those complexities and therefore is super useful.

A tip I'd offer too is that supermarkets do crustless quiches these days, and if you're not inclined to do the cooking, that's a way of getting quiche into your diet in diabetically friendly way.

I associate quiche with the summer, not exclusively, because quiche from the oven with vegetables on the side is a fab autumn and winter meal, but there is a whole set of them which are apt for summer al fresco dining. This recipe fits there.

Makes 8 slices

Ingredients

1 packet of readymade filo pastry (you will not need all of it)
30g butter
20ml sunflower oil
Half a head of broccoli
150g fillet of salmon

LIFE FOOD

3 eggs (free range)
150 ml single cream
Salt & white pepper
Tarragon (dried or fresh)

Method

Start by preparing the filling. The broccoli and salmon need to be cooked before going in the quiche, so first wash the broccoli and discard its woody parts, then cut the rest up into small pieces, keeping the florets intact, but small. Put this into a small saucepan with 2-3cm boiling water in it and steam for about 8 minutes. You want the broccoli still bright green and only just cooked. Take off the heat, drain, run cold water over the broccoli, drain again, and leave to dry and cool.

Put the salmon, skin side down, in a small pan with a little water, and cover with a lid. Heat to medium and lightly poach for about 5 minutes, take off the heat, and allow to cool slightly. Remove the fish to a plate and flake it, removing the skin. Put aside.

It's time to prepare the filo crust for the quiche. First of all, get an appropriate dish for the quiche: a wide and shallow dish which is about 25cm in diameter, and 2cm deep.

You're going to be brushing the filo sheets with the sunflower oil and butter, so melt the butter in a small bowl (easiest is microwaving) and then mix in the oil. Get a pastry brush at the ready.

Also make some space. You need a space to lay the filo sheets out, fully unwrapped. You need a space to work on the filo sheets individually. You need your quiche dish nearby.

Working with filo requires a little bit of skill and care. The pastry sheets are so thin that once they are opened and unwrapped they dry and thus get brittle incredibly quickly and can't be used. This means you have to work fast. Also, you need to protect the sheets while you are working. To do this you need 2 freshly cleaned tea towels that you have dampened. Open the filo and carefully cut open the inner cellophane wrapping. You are not going to use a full packet for the quiche, so you will be putting some of the filo back: it helps if it has been unwrapped neatly. The filo will be folded several times, so lay it on the first tea towel, and carefully unroll so that the sheets are open and flat. Lay the second tea towel on top. You're now ready to start working the filo. So, lifting the top tea towel, carefully lift a sheet of filo. Lay it on the space in front of you (which must be clear and clean). Cover the unused filo up again. Brush the entire surface of the filo sheet with a light layer of the oil and butter mixture. Once it is entirely covered, lift the filo and place it across the quiche dish, pressing it into the corners. Some minimal overhang over the edges (1cm) is fine, but if there is more than that either cut or fold back into the dish so that there isn't too much excess. Repeat this with 5 sheets of filo, and with each one change the position / orientation of the sheet so that overall everything overlaps. The objective is to ensure 100% of the dish is covered with filo.

Once you've done that, rewrap the unused filo and put it in the fridge to use for something else.

Unlike when you're using standard pastry you don't need to pre-cook the filo pastry, so as soon as the filo sheets are in, you are ready to put in the filling.

Start by placing the broccoli on top of the filo pastry, spreading it around evenly, and positioning the florets so they are upwards facing. Then scatter the salmon pieces around, also evenly, between the broccoli.

Then make the custard for the quiche: in a bowl, break the 3 eggs, and pour in the cream. Whisk this with a fork, sprinkle in the tarragon, and season with the salt and pepper. Pour this over the broccoli and salmon steadily.

LIFE FOOD

When I do this, I like to put the quiche dish on a baking sheet before I start to make the quiche, as its easier to manoeuvre in and out of the oven when the quiche is full of egg mixture. It also means that if there's any overspill as the quiche cooks you don't end up with it all over your oven.

Put the quiche into a pre-heated oven at 170° C / 340° F / Gas mark 3, and cook for 35-40 minutes.

When it is finished it will be slightly brown on top, the filo around the edges will definitely be browned, and the quiche filling will be slightly wobbly. Do make sure it is firm enough though and if it needs a bit more time in the oven, leave it for 5 more minutes.

Take it out, and allow it to cool somewhat before you serve because it will firm up a touch and be easier to take out of the dish and slice. Personally, I prefer this served warm to hot.

There are loads of alternative fillings you might go with instead of the broccoli and salmon. Here are a few ideas:

- Leek and sour cream – pre-cook sliced leeks, and replace the single cream with sour cream.
- Cherry tomato and black olive – cut the tomatoes in half.
- Cheddar and onion – grate cheddar into the custard, and mix sliced spring onions into it.
- Blue cheese and walnut – crumble stilton or similar into the custard, and mix chopped walnuts into it.
- Mushroom, goats' cheese and thyme – sauté sliced mushrooms (300g) for a few minutes and cook off / drain off any liquid, then crumble soft goats' cheese over it and add chopped fresh thyme to the custard.
- Roasted butternut and spinach – roast small cubes of butternut squash for 30 minutes, cool and add to the pastry case. Scatter a handful of clean baby spinach leaves over and add the custard. Also nice with cheddar added.

- 'Spanish' quiche – inspired by a Spanish omelette, this has halved cherry tomatoes, diced red onion, and chopped red and green pepper, topped with the custard and some cheddar.

A note on the leftover filo: I don't like making something and not having some ideas for what I might use the leftover filo for. Depending on the size of the packet you'll probably have 4-6 sheets left. Officially you should refrigerate and use within 3 days. I think as long as you use it within a week, maybe even more, you'll be fine.

LIFE FOOD

Gish's lentil quiche

Gish is a lovely woman who I think of fondly. It's funny how even though I haven't seen her in years, her kind explanation of how she made her lentil quiche stays with me, and is much treasured. I have already explained how much I like a good quiche, and Gish's contains lentils! Talk about a marriage made in heaven.

This is a completely different food to the salmon and broccoli filo quiche in this book. It is much heavier, made with a shortcrust pastry, and because the filling includes lentils, the quiche as a whole contains a lot of carbs. As a result, this gets served with low-carb sides such as green veg, broccoli, cabbage, leeks, spinach, courgettes, kale, salad leaves, and cauliflower.

It is a great meal for me though, combining carbs, fibre, and protein, and I like that the leftovers have the great secondary benefits of being delicious cold and travelling well for a work lunch or a picnic if we're out for a walk or an outing.

Serves: makes 8 generous slices.

Ingredients

1 onion
2 sticks celery
200g red lentils
3 garlic cloves, crushed
1 dessert spoon tomato puree
1 bay leaf
2 teaspoon herbes de Provence
1 large ripe tomato
4 eggs (free range)
150 ml single cream
Salt and black pepper

300g wholemeal flour

THE ABLE DIABETIC

150g vegetable shortening
Salt

<u>Method</u>

Make this in a fairly deep quiche dish, 25cm wide and 6cm deep.

Start by making the pastry so that it can rest for at least 30 minutes before being rolled out. Combine the flour, a pinch of salt, and the vegetable shortening in a large bowl, and rub the fat into the flour until it resembles breadcrumbs. Alternatively, pulse these ingredients in a food processor until breadcrumb texture. Add about 150ml cold water little by little to the breadcrumb mixture, pressing the dough together as you do it, until you have a firm dough. Try not to overdo the water because you don't want it to get sticky. Once the pastry dough is all together, leave it in a cool place for at least 30 minutes to allow the pastry to strengthen its gluten bonds.

To make the lentil filling, wash the lentils. Heat the sunflower oil in a large sauté pan and add the chopped onion and celery and cook until translucent. Add the lentils, crushed garlic, bay leaf, herbs, tomato puree, and just enough boiling water to cover and simmer until the lentils are cooked, which will take about 20-25 minutes. You will not be draining them, and you might have to add boiling water as you go along, but in the end you want no water remaining, so you have fully cooked but pulpy lentils. The only thing you remove once cooked is the bay leaf. Allow the lentils to cool.

Roll out the pastry, and carefully line the quiche dish with it. Leave some pastry overhanging (1cm). Prick the pastry all over with a fork, and cover fully with foil. Pour some baking beans on top of the foil, and put the pastry in a pre-heated oven at 180° C / 350° F / Gas mark 4. Cook for 15 minutes, until the pastry is just starting to have the edge of crispness. Take it out of the oven and ideally let it cool for 15 minutes. Remove the foil and baking beans.

Make the custard for the quiche by combining the eggs, cream, and salt and pepper and whisking them all together.

Assemble the quiche just before putting it back in the oven, by spreading the lentil mixture over the base, and pouring on the egg mixture. Lastly, slice the tomato into about 6 slices and lay them over the surface of the egg. Pop immediately into the oven, at 180° C / 350° F / Gas mark 4, and cook for 40 minutes. If the quiche still looks a bit under browned at that point give it a bit longer. This is quite a deep quiche, and the cooking time will vary depending on the dish used, so extend the cooking time if needed.

Take the quiche out of the oven. You can eat it immediately hot, or warm is lovely too. Serve with your chosen vegetables.

And some other ideas:

The lentil base can be mixed up easily to ring the changes to this recipe.

The quiche has a bit of a South of France vibe with the tomato and herbs de Provence, and so some delicious optional extras are black olives, sundried tomatoes, red onion slices, and anchovies. Some chopped up peppers would also give a nice extra dimension.

Completely alternatively, instead of the bay and the herbs de Provence, adding some curry powder and red chilli to the lentils and then put fresh coriander in the egg custard. Wonderful too.

Last but not least, a lot of quiches have cheese in them, and adding cheddar, goats' cheese, or something like red Leicester will all work. I love cheese and eat too much of it, so I try to stick without it, but it's a personal choice.

Rainbow noodles

It would be a sad world without noodles. While I'm all for manners around food, the slurpiness of noodles gives them a special place all of their own. Noodle based food does come with the risk that the carbs will take over though, and so this recipe is designed to balance the carbs out with a lot of veg.

The name found its way into our lexicon when the children were young and 'non-vegetable' branding helped with food adoption. Both our children were entirely unfussy, so that's no slight on them: they just enjoyed the joy of these being rainbow-like.

The rainbow noodles name also meant that the veg involved didn't have to be exactly the same every time, as long as it was colourful. I like that latitude. My aim is to include as many different colours as I can manage, keeping things practical.

Serves 4

Ingredients:

250g pack of egg noodles (dry; uncooked)

Glug of sunflower oil
2cm piece of fresh ginger, peeled and sliced into tiny pieces
4 cloves garlic – peeled and crushed
1 yellow pepper – deseeded and sliced thinly
1 red pepper – deseeded and sliced thinly
1 orange pepper – deseeded and sliced thinly
1 carrot – peeled and sliced into long thin pieces / made into ribbons with a peeler
1 courgette – sliced into long thin pieces / made into ribbons with a peeler
¼ red cabbage – shredded finely
¼ broccoli head – florets cut off into bite sized pieces, and the stem peeled and sliced into thin lengths

LIFE FOOD

6 spring onions – washed well, the ends cut off, then cut into small pieces

1 tablespoon dark soy sauce
1 tablespoon oil, either flavourless like sunflower, or toasted sesame
1 tablespoon rice vinegar
½ tablespoon honey
1 red chilli sliced

Bunch coriander – washed, leaves pulled off, and stalks diced into small pieces

Method

This recipe is all about the vegetable prep, so do that first, getting everything sliced as above and ready so that the cooking time will be super quick.

Make the dressing, by putting the soy sauce, oil, rice vinegar, honey and sliced chilli in a bowl and whisking it until it is smooth and fully combined.

It will take about 10 minutes start to finish to make this, so when you're close to the time you want to eat, get a pan of boiling water and add the noodles. Keep the pan on the hob but turn the heat off after 30 seconds and let the noodles cook. This will take about 4 minutes. Once cooked, drain immediately and leave to the side.

Meanwhile, working in parallel to the noodles cooking, heat up a wok or similar pan on the hob, to a medium high heat, and add a large glug of sunflower oil. After a few seconds, add the harder veg – the cabbage, broccoli, and cook for 1 minute. Then add all the rest of the veg except the spring onions (peppers, carrot, courgettes), plus the prepared garlic and ginger, and cook for 3-5 minutes. The veg should be just cooked, and the colour should still be vibrant. Take this off the hob.

THE ABLE DIABETIC

Now stir the noodles through the vegetables, and pour over the dressing. Transfer to plates or a big serving dish, sprinkle the chopped spring onions over, and then the coriander. You're ready to serve and enjoy.

Spinach and brown rice bake

I found this recipe when faced with the very large bag of brown rice my dad bought me when I was at uni. It originally came from a Delia Smith recipe. Great though it was, there were pros and cons once I became type 1. The main components, brown rice, spinach, eggs are all great, but the original recipe contained a lot of brown rice making it too carb laden for me. So, this recipe has been on a bit of a journey with me to make it much more t1d friendly.

The basic dish is cooked rice + eggs + cheese + spinach + some warming spice. My changes are to increase the veg, replace some of the rice with green lentils, and decrease the rest of the rice to a level that works for me.

This is a great make-ahead meal, and if people are going to be eating at different times you can use individual dishes for the portions, which makes it a superbly practical family meal.

Serves 4-6

Ingredients

Sunflower oil
10g butter
1 onion, diced
2 sticks celery, washed and chopped
2 leeks, well washed and sliced
150g brown basmati rice
50g green lentils
450ml of hot stock (vegetable or chicken) or hot water
500g of spinach leaves
1 courgette
4-5 spring onions
100g cheddar cheese, grated
3 eggs, free range
Salt and black pepper

½ -1 teaspoon grated nutmeg
1 slice wholemeal seeded bread made into crumbs
50g mixed seeds
30g cheddar, grated

Method

You will need a large ovenproof dish about 25cm x 20cm which you've pre-oiled, or 4 individual dishes.

Start with a large saucepan on a medium heat and add the sunflower oil and butter, and allow to melt. Add the diced onion, chopped up celery, and cook until translucent, then add the leeks and cook for 2 more minutes.

Into that add the brown basmati and green lentils, both of which should have been washed, stir to coat in the oil and vegetables, and then add the stock or pre-boiled water. The rice will take about 40 minutes to cook, on a low simmer, with the lid on the saucepan, and occasionally stirred.

Meanwhile prepare the spinach by washing, picking through, and chopping, and chop up the courgette into small pieces. Ten minutes before the rice is due to be finished cooking, stir in the courgettes.

Take the saucepan off the heat, and let it cool for at least 15 minutes. The rice mixture needs to be well cooled before adding the eggs because you don't want them cooking from the residual heat.

The next stage is to mix the chopped spinach, grated cheddar, and whisked eggs to the rice and to mix round well. Lastly, add salt, ground black pepper, and the nutmeg and stir through.

Transfer the rice, veg and egg mixture to the prepared oven dish and then sprinkle the breadcrumbs mixed with the seeds and the 30g of cheddar over the top.

LIFE FOOD

Bake in the oven at 180° C / 350° F / Gas mark 4 for about 35-40 minutes, until the bake has puffed up and the top is browned.

Goes well with a tomato salad.

Mackerel and tomato pasta

I have a strong preference for eating mackerel over other fish because it's heart-healthy and it is also wild and caught close to the UK coast. I find it pretty hard to buy fish products that live up to my standards. As it's important health-wise to eat oily fish, mackerel features quite a lot in our home, usually once a week.

This particular recipe is a huge favourite. It is asked for above all other pasta recipes. It's so easy, the children learnt to cook it themselves before most other things. It also takes only the time the pasta takes to cook from start to finish, i.e. about 10 minutes. Literally.

In terms of health credentials, we don't eat this with wholewheat pasta, but it's a robust enough recipe to complement wholewheat well, so do go ahead and do that.

Although I struggle with pasta based meals, by which I mean that a large plate of pasta with just a cream sauce or not much in the way of veggies does drag me in the direction of over-eating carbs, this recipe is pretty good. It's important that the pasta is balanced out by plenty of veg & protein otherwise the plate of starch I end up eating results in a massive blood glucose peak. Also, it has been shown now that eating some salad or veg in advance of your carbs helps to limit the impact of the carbs on your blood sugar, especially the speed with which it increases, and so it's good for a t1d to bear in mind that every mouthful that isn't pasta at the start of the meal, helps.

Serves 4

Ingredients

400g of pasta – spaghetti or penne
300g of smoked mackerel fillets (we prefer peppered)
4 fresh tomatoes
A generous sprinkle of chilli flakes

LIFE FOOD

1 lemon
150ml crème fraiche

Method

Start by putting on the water to boil. As soon as it is boiling put the dry pasta in.

In a bowl suitable for mixing the sauce, start with the mackerel fillets, and take off the skin, discard, and shred the mackerel into smallish pieces.

Then wash the tomatoes, and dice them into small pieces, and put into the bowl with the mackerel.

Next, juice the lemon, and pour it all over the mackerel and tomatoes in the bowl. (You can wash the lemon's skin too and get some lemon zest if you want, and add to the final dish).

Sprinkle the chilli flakes over. Then add the generous dollop of crème fraiche on top too, and stir everything together. All of that takes about 4 minutes, so you'll have it finished a few minutes before the pasta is cooked!

Once cooked, drain the pasta, and, off the heat, transfer the mackerel mixture from the bowl to the pan and stir until well combined.

Serve into pasta bowls. If you saved some lemon zest, sprinkle it over.

I recommend that you serve with the option of adding more chilli flakes individually, and for this reason, think it's best to hold back on the amount of chilli flakes in the sauce, just in case it's too much for anyone.

Enjoy!

Lauren's cayenne chicken farfalle

My daughter has been a talented and capable cook since she was quite young. Her cakes are excellent – she has a lighter hand than I do. Since she's been at university and feeding herself, I've been constantly impressed by her ability to buy sensibly and eat thoroughly well on her limited budget.

We often swap food pictures, and recently a photo of this recipe appeared on my phone. It had been a bit of an experiment but turned out scrumptious. So, I asked if I could steal it for this book, and she gave me her blessing!

I recommend wholewheat pasta. To be honest we don't eat wholewheat pasta a lot. I know it is better for you, but overall, I don't worry about our vegetable and fibre intake, and in most cases I think standard pasta is a lot less intrusive from a flavour and texture perspective. That's the honest truth. However, when a pasta dish is robust and packs a flavour punch, wholewheat pasta works, and this pasta sauce certainly delivers on the flavour front.

Serves 4

Ingredients

300g farfalle or other pasta shapes (wholewheat ideally)
Glug of olive oil
300g punnet of cherry tomatoes
1 red onion
250g of cooked chicken
½ teaspoon cayenne pepper
½ round of Boursin cheese (garlic and herb) – or similar

Method

In a large saucepan, boil 2 litres of water, and put the pasta on to cook.

LIFE FOOD

While it is cooking, in another small saucepan, at a medium heat, add a glug of olive oil, and the sliced red onion and cook briefly, then add the washed cherry tomatoes and let them heat up so that they burst and collapse. Add the chicken pieces and let them warm through thoroughly. Add the cayenne pepper.

When the pasta is ready, drain it well, and stir the sauce and the Boursin cheese into it. Stir until all fully distributed.

Serve immediately.

A nice addition to this dish would be 400g of fresh leaf spinach, well washed, and added to the cooked pasta along with the sauce. Spinach complements the sauce and increases the nutritional value.

THE ABLE DIABETIC

Sausage & borlotti bean casserole

My ethical position on food has moved a lot over the last 15 years, and influenced the way my family eats a great deal. It's not that I didn't care before, but the level of concern has ramped up. I am 100% in favour of the nose-to-tail ethos of eating meat, and think that we absolutely should eat every bit of an animal. I'm also, to be candid, a bit sniffy about people who will only eat the cuts of meat they fancy; it's not a favourite attitude of mine. I firmly believe if you're going to eat meat you should respect the animal you're eating.

Having said all of that, I don't find it easy. To my shame, I would struggle to eat a plate of liver and onions. When I was a child tongue sandwiches sometimes made an appearance in the houses of the older generation and I found it repulsive, and still do. Don't even mention sweetbreads (yes, brains!). So, I'm not on strong ground when it comes to lecturing. But I will eat offal if it's 'packaged' in a way I find acceptable, which includes liver pâté for example, black pudding, and then the entire array of salamis and sausages that exist in the UK and especially Europe. Frankly, I think the disguise is pure genius.

And of course, sausages fall squarely in this category, and so are the easiest way to assuage my conscience around my moral obligation to eat offal and also put something which will be scoffed with no questions on the table. Again, I have my standards, and so the sausages that we typically eat at home come from pigs that have led happy outdoor lives.

I also try to make sausages go a long way. This is a good thing for environmental and health considerations, and happily, sits well with the principles that underpin my t1d cooking too: there is nothing bad about reducing the sausage amount in a meal and replacing it with vegetables and pulses. Which brings us to this sausage casserole. I put 6 sausages in this as standard. If I were to serve the men in the family 1.5 sausages alongside a pile of mash there would be rebellion! Served in the casserole, there won't be a squeak. I'm

LIFE FOOD

sure there have been times when I've taken it down to 4.... the secret is out!

I've just mentioned mash, and I would serve this with some mashed potato. With the vegetables and pulses in the casserole, it's totally alright for me to have a small amount on the side.

Serves 4

Ingredients

Glug of sunflower oil
1 large onion, chopped
1 stick celery, chopped small
6 sausages, total weight about 400g
3 cloves garlic, crushed
1 leek, washed and sliced
300g mushrooms, cleaned and sliced
1 large courgette
1 400g tin borlotti beans
50g puy style lentils (lentilles vertes)
1 400g tin chopped tomatoes
Glug extra virgin olive oil
1 bay leaf
A few stalks fresh rosemary, cut into small pieces
Salt & black pepper

Method

I make this in a 22cm casserole dish which is useable on the hob and in the oven, and which is about 3 litres volume.

Put the casserole dish on the hob and heat up the glug of sunflower oil at a medium heat, then add the chopped onion and celery, and cook for about 3-5 minutes.

THE ABLE DIABETIC

Cut the sausages up into chunks, each sausage into 4-5 pieces, and add to the pan. I use kitchen scissors and cut straight into the pan. Let the sausages start to brown, moving them around a bit as you go. Don't move them too much as that will stop them from browning.

Then add the crushed garlic, the washed and sliced leek, the cleaned and sliced mushrooms, and the chopped courgette, and cook for a minute or so.

Pour in the chopped tomatoes, the bay leaf and the chopped rosemary. Add the rinsed and drained borlotti beans. Add the puy lentils/ lentilles vertes. Put the lid on the casserole dish and let the whole casserole simmer gently for 40 minutes. The veg will give off moisture and so it is unlikely you'll need to add water, but if things are looking too dry, pour in some pre-boiled water.

In the meantime, make any side dishes. I would make mash, and possibly a green veg, just because the more you eat the better!

When the casserole is cooked, pour a small glug of olive oil into it, which just enhances the fragrance and feel of it. And season, or let people do that themselves.

If you cool and reheat the casserole, it will taste even better.

Bean burgers and sweet potato fries

Fast food has never been a thing for me, thank goodness. But a long time ago, in the USA, I discovered Burger King's spicy bean burger, and it was the fast food item I actually liked. Apparently the spicy bean burger was removed from the BK menu years ago and was relaunched in January 2024 to respond to Vegan January. Anyhow, I have long imitated the BK spicy bean burgers, and so have experimented with a variety of things to get to some that I rate highly.

Like pretty much everyone else, my family like a good burger meal. The classic combo of meat burger + burger bun + chips on the side is not great for me as a t1d. The chips AND burger bun is a lot of carbs. They're essentially just white starch and don't deliver much nutritional value. Not worth it. By having the burger made primarily from pulses, it becomes "good" veg-based carbs, and I serve it with chunky sweet potato fries because they are much more nutritious and lower GI. The bun is not welcome, but I like to have it (sometimes). Served with a nice side salad, there is plenty of food joy here.

Serves 4

Ingredients

1 400g tin black beans
1 400g tin kidney beans
1 red pepper – finely diced
1 red onion – finely diced
80g breadcrumbs, preferably wholemeal
1 egg, free range
1 teaspoon smoked paprika
1 teaspoon cumin
½ teaspoon cayenne pepper
Juice from 1 lime
Salt and pepper

THE ABLE DIABETIC

4 medium sweet potatoes
Glug of sunflower oil

Lettuce – 1 sweet gem or similar
300g punnet of cherry tomatoes
1 small red onion
1 medium avocado
Another lime

Method

It is best I think if the bean burger mix is made a couple of hours in advance as it all seems to come together better then. In a largish food prep bowl, put the drained and rinsed beans and squish into a roughish paste with a fork. The level to which you mash things here dictates a lot of the ultimate texture of the burgers, so don't mash too finely, but it does need to be a paste.

To this mixture add these other ingredients: the breadcrumbs, red pepper dice and red onion dice, the smoked paprika, cumin, cayenne, salt & pepper, and the egg, and then mix it all up. The mixture should be quite firm, and you want it to be so. The last ingredient to add is the lime juice and while you want the burger mixture to be workable into patties, you don't want it too wet. So, add with care. Then divide the mixture into 4 equally sized portions, and shape into fat burger shapes, about 2cm thick. Leave somewhere cool (or in the fridge if more than an hour or two).

About an hour ahead of when you want to serve the meal, prep the sweet potato fries. Put the oven on to 180° C / 350° F / Gas mark 4. Peel the sweet potatoes and cut them into large wedges – I would recommend making about 4-6 per sweet potato. In a bowl, coat the wedges in sunflower oil (you don't need much). Transfer to a baking tray and put in the oven. They'll need about 45 minutes to cook and go the nice blend of crispy and fudgy that you get with this vegetable.

LIFE FOOD

The bean burgers will take 20 minutes to cook from room temperature. In a sauté pan which is large enough to accommodate all 4 patties, add a small amount of sunflower oil, and add the burgers to the pan. Leave 1-2 cm between each of them. Cook over a medium heat – you want to cook the middles thoroughly and also develop a crust on the outside of the burger. To achieve this do not move the burgers for about 8-10 minutes, then using a fish slice, carefully turn each burger patty over. Then leave the patties untouched for the remaining 10 or so minutes of cooking time.

While the food cooks, prepare the salad, washing and cutting up the lettuce, and and dicing the red onion. Scoop the avocado flesh out, dice it, and squeeze the lime juice over it. Scatter over the salad, and dress with a little olive oil.

You're ready to serve!

In our home, whatever burger gets produced, with whatever sides, Heinz ketchup is still a requirement. I don't have it, but I don't judge if you do!

THE ABLE DIABETIC

Spicy Ricey

This recipe is written down in my handwritten book of recipes, in Lauren's handwriting. She has written the date: April 29th. I just wish I knew which year, but I'm guessing probably about 2012 or 2013 when she would have been 7 or 8. The name was an invention of the children's.

I considered putting Jambalaya in this book, because that's a recipe that Jim has fond travel-related memories of, but Spicy Ricey is our more homespun, similar, rice-based meal. I'm including it because the kids loved it, it's characterised by the adaptive approach of this book generally, and that link back to Lauren is assuredly special.

This recipe has rice in it, but red lentils too, and a lot of different types of vegetable. It's family friendly, but also tasty enough for the grownups to enjoy. Possibly with a dash of tabasco.

Ingredients

2 onions, diced
Two sticks of celery, diced
5 cloves garlic, minced
4 rashers bacon
Glug of sunflower oil
3 large carrots, peeled and diced
2 400g tins chopped tomatoes
1 courgette, chopped
1 red pepper, chopped
1 green pepper, chopped
100g of red lentils
100g of long grain rice
1 400g tin kidney beans
½ teaspoon chilli flakes

LIFE FOOD

<u>Method</u>

This is a pure one pot meal. You need a large 2-3 litre saucepan.

Warm up the saucepan on the hob and add a glug of sunflower oil. Add the onion and the celery, and cook for 2 minutes. Then cut up the bacon and put that in the saucepan, with the minced garlic cloves. Keep cooking this for a few minutes until the bacon is cooked but not brown.

Add the carrots, peppers, and courgettes to the saucepan. Put the lid on top. Then add the tinned tomatoes.

Wash the lentils and rice, and then put those in the pan. Pour over enough boiling water from a kettle to cover the rice plus 1 cm. Lastly, drain and rinse the kidney beans and add them too.

All of this will cook on the hob in about 30 minutes, needing an occasional stir. Don't stir frequently because that will break up the rice, distribute its starch and make the dish sticky, but do ensure it isn't sticking to the base of the pan. When the rice is cooked, its ready to eat straight away. A wholesome and filling family meal.

N.B. You can add the chilli flakes when you add the tinned tomatoes, or leave it for people to do it as they eat. The fact that the chilli is the last ingredient in Lauren's list suggests it wasn't added to the meal as it cooked because Greg would have been very young (3ish).

Kedgeree

This is another meal my children love. Surprising for Greg, in particular. He really doesn't like eggs. Doesn't much like fish. Loves kedgeree. Work that out.

I get it though – kedgeree is an unusual dish. It's a surprise that curry, smoked fish, and eggs can end up being so delicious. Even more surprising that this was originally invented as a breakfast dish. But there you go.

My version is different to the classic one for two reasons. I use smoked mackerel not smoked haddock for both health (oily fish) and environmental reasons, and I add a few lentils to the rice for health (fibre, protein) reasons. I've waxed lyrical about mackerel before, and this is another recipe that I've found carries smoked mackerel superbly. At the end of the day, this is a straightforward and simple dish, and you can mess with it in all kinds of ways and still end up with something yummy and good for you. All of the ingredients are swappable.

Serves 4

Ingredients

200g rice (I use white or brown basmati) most of the time; you need unsticky long grain
4 eggs, free range
350g smoked mackerel
1 onion, diced
Glug of sunflower oil
2 teaspoons medium curry powder
400g tin green lentils
300g frozen peas
A little butter and / or cream to finish
1 lemon, quartered

LIFE FOOD

Method

The rice and the eggs need to be cooked before you can start to prepare the actual kedgeree. I tend to do this in advance.

Cook the rice according to your usual method, and when it is done, let it cool. It is also fine to transfer the just cooked rice to the kedgeree after you've started preparing it.

Separately, boil the eggs, until you have them as hard as your preference. I try to make them halfway between soft and hard, so they are a bit jammy, about 7-8 minutes for medium eggs. Once cooked, allow to cool at least to the point they are handleable, and take the shells off.

To make the kedgeree itself, start with a wide sauté or wok style pan and heat it to a medium heat on the hob. Add the glug of sunflower oil, and then the diced onion, and cook until translucent. Then add the curry spices and fry for a couple of minutes until the fragrance is released.

At this point add the rice, and move it around until it is hot. I put a little water in the pan and cover the entire pan to steam the rice – it seems to help with the rice sticking to the bottom of the pan. You do have to be a bit careful because you don't want the rice broken up or mushy.

When the rice is hot, stir in the drained and rinsed lentils, and the frozen peas. Cover again so that the peas thaw and get hot.

Meanwhile, take the skin off the smoked mackerel, flake it into pieces, and remove any bones you can see. Then add the mackerel pieces to the pan and stir through, so they can warm.

The kedgeree is now ready. It will happily sit for a few minutes. If you're going to add butter and cream, stir them in to mix through the whole dish. Although these add fat, they finish the dish off nicely.

The kedgeree can be served individually but I like it piled on a platter with the eggs, quartered, placed around on top. It looks very pretty and quite grand!

Last but not least, give everyone a quarter of a lemon to squeeze over the kedgeree before they eat. It too adds a little something.

LIFE FOOD

Carpenter's pie

I once did a short consulting job that introduced me to Spike Milligan's widow, Shelagh Sinclair. People remember him for his unique wit, but he was also a keen environmentalist and vegetarian, and they had this in common. She was advising on a vegetarian menu when I met her.

This recipe is based on something she developed, and while this recipe is mine not hers, I've kept the name. I hope she wouldn't mind me nicking it. I doubt if she would. She was a warm, friendly and generous spirited lady, all about the mission to encourage people to eat veggie food, and somehow managed to do it without being at all lecturing, just inclusive and optimistic. I offer it here in that spirit, a kind of paying it forward.

I have introduced a definite difference in my recipe which is is to switch up the mash from being potato based to a mix of potatoes and butter beans. For me, pies that have a potato topping verge into the danger zone, and while a t1d can eat them – of course – there is the risk of overdoing the carb load. This switch increases the protein and decreases the carb, and makes this just a bit easier.

The meal benefits from a straightforward, colourful, vegetable side because, while delicious, it is very brown!

Serves 4

Ingredients

Glug of sunflower oil
1 large onion, diced
4 cloves garlic, crushed
800g of mushrooms, ideally a combination of chestnut, portobello / flat, and baby mushrooms
1 teaspoon Marmite

THE ABLE DIABETIC

Splash of dark soy sauce
2 heaped teaspoons of onion gravy granules (e.g. Bisto)
1 dessert spoon of fresh thyme, chopped
400g potatoes, a floury variety
1x 400g tin butterbeans
100g cheddar, grated
Milk
Salt and white pepper

Method

You will need a large, deep ovenproof dish, approx. 30cm x 20cm.

To make the pie filling, warm a glug of sunflower oil in a medium saucepan and add the diced onion. Sauté for a few minutes until translucent and starting to brown slightly.

Prepare the mushrooms by cleaning them, slicing the large ones, and halving the chestnut ones. You want a range of shapes and sizes to give the filling an interesting texture. Add all the prepared mushrooms to the pan and then add the crushed garlic. Continue to cook on a gentle medium heat for about 5-8 minutes so that they have given up a fair bit of their juice.

Then add 200ml of boiled kettle water, still hot, and the onion gravy granules, 1 teaspoon marmite, and a good splash of soy sauce. Sprinkle on the chopped thyme. If you would like the gravy to be a bit thicker add a bit more of the gravy granules. Now set aside and cool slightly.

You can make the mash for the topping in parallel to making the mushroom filling. Start by peeling the potatoes and cutting them into large chunks. Put them in a suitable saucepan with a few centimetres of water, and with the lid on, steam them until they are tender, about 25 minutes. Rinse and drain the butterbeans and add to the potatoes for 5 further minutes. When you test the potatoes and they are tender, drain. then mash the potato and bean mixture

LIFE FOOD

to a smooth mash. I say smooth, my preference is not over smooth, as I think some texture is a nice thing here, and this is a rustic meal. Stir the grated cheddar in, add salt and pepper, and mix through well.

Assemble the pie by putting the mushroom filling in the ovenproof dish, and carefully dollop mash on top to fully cover it.

Bake in the oven at 180° C / 350° F / Gas mark 4 for 30 minutes (longer if from chilled).

THE ABLE DIABETIC

Halloumi kebabs and brown rice

My daughter loves kebabs and loves Halloumi, so these are for her. In general, she shares my love for food of the eastern Mediterranean. We eat these in the summer, when it is sunny, and you can sit outside.

I think kebabs are a brilliant way of combining protein and veg and they are inherently portion controlled which is a good thing for me. I like grilling food because of the smoky edge and the succulence in the middle too.

This style of food does come with a bit of a word of caution. Often kebabs are seen alongside a selection of mezze, with things like hummus, salads, other stewed vegetables and parcels of food, either in pastry or similar. All of the food just mentioned is super healthy and vibrant, but it is easy to lose track of what you've eaten, especially when a pile of bread is also served to accompany all the mezze. An experienced t1d will likely be able to work out what is in front of them, but it isn't easy. Hummus for example contains quite a lot of carbs. I find the best tip is to get yourself a full plate, i.e. everything you're going to eat, in one take and don't continue to graze after you've eaten. I am undoubtedly bad at this so struggle to practise what I preach. At the same time, I know I'm giving good advice, and I do try to follow it.

At home, I would keep this quite simple. Having a simple lettuce, tomato, cucumber salad helps me to fill my plate without relying too much on carbs, and I would include hummus but would add just a blob to my plate. The brown rice, in a controlled portion size, is an ideal thing to provide the carb quotient.

An alternative to the brown rice is tabbouleh, which is even more delicious.

Serves 4

LIFE FOOD

Ingredients

2 225g packs of halloumi (we like the one with chilli in it too)
2 red, green or yellow peppers
1 red onion
1 courgette
300g punnet cherry tomatoes
Olive oil
1 teaspoon each of chilli flakes, oregano, cumin

200g brown rice, dry weight

To serve:
Simple salad: lettuce, cucumber, tomato
Hummus
Extra virgin olive oil and lemon wedges

Method

If you're going to eat this straight away, start the rice first, cooking it gently per instructions.

Also prepare your salad and put to one side

To make the kebabs you will need 8 skewers 20cm long, or 4 of the 40cm barbeque length.

Prepare the kebab ingredients by cutting everything to a suitable size. Be careful not to make things too large because then they won't cook through, but also not too small because that increases the risk of them tearing and falling off the skewers. It takes a bit of judgement! The halloumi usually has a natural crack through it so work with that. Aim to cut the halloumi into cubes of about 1.5-2cm. For the peppers, deseed, and cut into 2cm squares. The courgette cut into discs about 1cm thick. For the red onion, take the skin off, cut off the root, and then cut into 1/6 wedges and separate into layers. Once you've done all that, divide each ingredient into 4, and thread onto each skewer, so that they are all composed in a similar way, with the different ingredients mixed up.

N.B. you can also tailor the kebabs to individual needs if someone doesn't like one of the ingredients.

Once the kebabs are made up, mix the olive oil with chilli flakes, cumin and oregano and brush liberally all over the kebabs.

Put the kebabs onto a grill tray and cook on a medium grill heat for about 15 minutes, turning when one side is cooked. Be careful not to burn yourself.

Perfect sunny food. Works well cooked on a barbeque.

LIFE FOOD

Green mac 'n' cheese

I have always loved the cheesy, rich, savoury delights of macaroni cheese. It is, however, a dish that I can't permit myself, because I eat too much of it – it is somehow just a meal that begs to be had more of - and it is simply not a health food. That's even before you get to the t1d part of the consideration, at which point something that is so fundamentally based on pasta becomes a real danger zone.

Into that situation came Farmer J's, a purveyor of wonderful food that I got introduced to when working in Shoreditch. They do tray food, which basically means a bit of a variety of things, and one of those is green mac 'n' cheese.

Now, the Farmer J's approach is one that is generally useful as a t1d: building your meal made of a spoonful of this and a spoonful of that allows you to achieve your personalised blend of veg + protein + carbs. Yes, you have to know what is in things, but it's pretty fab to be "allowed" something you couldn't have in bulk as a small part of the overall plate.

The other genius thing is that their mac 'n' cheese is green! Which simply means that lots of green veg is added to the basic recipe. Thank you Farmer J – I have taken this and run with it, and happily enjoy this marvellous meal now.

You can mix up the green veg. My preferred combo is in the recipe, but use what you like. You could even add something not green – gasp – although personally I struggle with that concept!

Serves 4, well

<u>Ingredients</u>

1 head of broccoli
2 leeks

THE ABLE DIABETIC

Spinach – either 200g fresh or frozen
150g frozen peas
1 bunch spring onions
300g dried macaroni pasta (or penne, rigatoni etc.)

Sauce:
75g butter
75g plain flour
750ml milk
Salt & white pepper
100g cheddar, ideally mature, grated

Wholemeal, ideally seedy, breadcrumbs

Method

You will need a large overproof dish, roughly 30cm x 20cm

Start by cooking the pasta as per the packet instructions, and once cooked, drain and put to one side.

Prepare the veg: wash and chop the broccoli and leeks into bite size piece. I trim the woody parts of the broccoli but use the stalk, diced into cubes. Waste not want not. Also chop the spring onions into small dice.

In a large, lidded saucepan, bring 2cm of water to the boil, and put in the broccoli and leeks. Cook for about 8 minutes, then add the peas, and fairly soon after turn off the heat and drain thoroughly. Add the spinach and spring onions, and let everything cook for 2 more minutes in the residual heat. Don't overcook the veg as it is going in the oven later.

Make the sauce in the usual way for white sauce. In a small saucepan, melt the butter, add the flour and combine to a paste (the roux), and then gradually whisk in the milk, ensuring that the sauce, as it thickens on the bottom of the pan, isn't allowed to stick and burn.

LIFE FOOD

The sauce needs to be cooked on a fairly high heat for several minutes until it is fully thickened. Once this is done, take it off the heat and add the cheese.

To assemble the dish, pour the hot cheese sauce over the macaroni in its saucepan, and combine well, then stir in the drained green veg.

Put all of this into the ovenproof dish.

I like to top this with a good sprinkling of brown or wholemeal breadcrumbs, even better if there are seeds in the mix, and a small grating of cheddar.

This goes into an oven at 180° C / 350° F / Gas mark 4, for 30 minutes, or until brown on top. You can also chill it after assembling and reheat, when it will take 45 minutes to cook. It's freezable as long as you put it in the freezer soon after it is made.

Nice served with a salad, but also nice served in a bowl, when it's cold outside, and the food warms not just your tummy but your soul.

Lamb and lentil moussaka

I don't eat a lot of lamb. It can be lovely, but it can also disappoint. I certainly prefer it in the food of the eastern Mediterranean spiced up a bit, often grilled, and complemented by zingy, herby, fresh flavours.

I also think lambs are imbued with joy, and seeing young lambs in fields in spring gives me so much pleasure as I watch their boinginess. I'm unquestionably sentimental about them. At those points, eating them feels so very sad. So, there are lots of reasons for lamb being a rare event in our home.

I do make an exception in my own kitchen for moussaka which is a dish I love. Something baked, rich, meaty, vegetably and savoury is right up my street. Originally I made moussaka in a classic way: the meat layered with potatoes, and aubergines with a bechamel topping. These days the recipe has been tweaked in the direction of a lot of my hallmarks: a lot less meat proportionately, the addition of pulses, and a lighter 'bechamel' made of yogurt.

As recipes go, this is a reasonably involved one as, before you assemble the thing, you have to make the lamb and lentil component, pre-cook the potatoes and aubergines, and pre-make the topping. It's not an everyday thing, but it is always much enjoyed when we have it.

Serves 8

For the lamb and lentil tomato sauce:

Ingredients

Glug of olive oil
500g minced lamb
2 400g tins chopped tomatoes

LIFE FOOD

2 onions
5 cloves garlic, minced
3 sticks celery, chopped small
75g red lentils (washed)
75g green lentils (washed)
1 teaspoon cinnamon
1 teaspoon cumin
1 teaspoon thyme
½ teaspoon ground ginger
½ teaspoon ground nutmeg
Vegetable stock

Method

In a wide-bottomed saucepan, start with a glug of olive oil, and a medium heat, and add the chopped onions and chopped celery and sauté until translucent. Then add the minced lamb and cook until brown. Just before the end of this process, add the garlic, and the spices - cinnamon, cumin, ginger and nutmeg.

Then add the tins of chopped tomatoes, the red and green lentils, the thyme and oregano and the stock. Simmer this for 30 minutes and take off the hob. Let it cool a little.

For the potato and aubergine layers:

Ingredients

900g large potatoes
2 aubergines

Method

The potatoes and aubergines need to be pre-cooked.

THE ABLE DIABETIC

Peel the potatoes, and par boil until just tender. Drain them and let them cool down, then slice into rounds of 5mm / half a cm thick. Wash the aubergines, cut of the stalk end and discard, and cut them into long slices (you can do rounds, but I prefer lengthwise) about 7mm thick, and place on a baking tray. Drizzle with a little olive oil (they absorb a lot so don't be too liberal!), and bake for 15 minutes by which time they will be soft and a little toasted around the edges. You don't want crisps so take care.

For the white sauce topping:

Ingredients

500g Greek yogurt
3 eggs
100g cheddar cheese, grated

Method

If you would prefer to use a white bechamel sauce go ahead, but I like this yogurt based topping. It's a bit lighter, and is super-easy to put together.

You literally combine the three ingredients, all cold, in a bowl, and stir them together until fully combined.

Assembling the moussaka:

You'll need a large, ovenproof dish with a 2 litre capacity.

The objective in the assembling is to do layers in this order: meat sauce, then aubergine, then potatoes, with 2 sets of both (i.e. 6 layers in total). If your dish doesn't quite work with this, you may wish to make fewer or more layers.

For 2 layers, start by putting ½ the meat mixture in the dish and make level. Then place ½ of your aubergine slices over the top of the meat, laying them in such a way that they are evenly placed. On top of the aubergines, do the same with ½ of the potatoes. After the potatoes, do another layer of meat mixture, then the rest of the aubergines, and then the rest of the potatoes. At this point all of those should be used up.

The final preparation step is to spread the white sauce topping over the top layer of potatoes.

The moussaka is now ready to bake, and can happily stand and wait in the fridge for a couple of days if it is covered.

When wanted, put into an oven at 170° C and bake for an hour. Extend the time if it is a deeper dish. By the time it comes out the topping should be attractively browned.

This is a pretty hefty meal and so I like to serve it with a large green salad, and potentially a Greek salad without the feta (i.e. cucumber, tomatoes, red onion, black olives, oregano, olive oil and lemon juice).

THE ABLE DIABETIC

Sweet potato and feta parcels

This recipe was originally made, and I think invented, by Lauren and I. Certainly it is written down in Lauren's handwriting and has hearts drawn next to it. She would have been in her early teens when it came into being.

It makes me smile to see it written down because there are a few things about it that are very "us". The fact this uses filo. The fact the filling includes beans. The feta + red onion + sweet potato combo aligns with Lauren, being her favourite kinds of flavours. And yet this recipe would probably be made with butternut squash except for the fact that Greg doesn't like it, so I think the sweet potato would originally have been a substitute choice.

I am sure this recipe is here not because we were aiming to make food that was for type 1 diabetics but that it sounded like good food. However, the recipe is a kind of proof point that my way of cooking has become woven into our family ways.

This recipe uses filo pastry which takes a little skill and experience to handle confidently. I give detailed instructions on how to use filo pastry in the recipe for Salmon and Broccoli filo quiche, also in this section of the book, so have a read of that if you're not confident.

It's served with a salad on the side, and is an ideal meal for me.

Serves 4

Ingredients

1 270g pack filo pastry
1 sweet potato, peeled and grated
1 red onion, finely chopped
2 garlic cloves
1 400g tin cannellini beans
200g feta cheese

LIFE FOOD

1 tablespoon chopped mint
2 tablespoons rapeseed oil
Salt and black pepper

<u>Salad dressing</u>
2 tablespoon white wine vinegar
1 spoon wholegrain mustard
1 teaspoon honey
Orange juice
Rapeseed oil
Salt & black pepper

Soft lettuce, e.g. English round lettuce, washed and leaves separated
½ a red onion, sliced
300g punnet of cherry tomatoes, washed and halved

<u>Method</u>

Start by preparing the stuffing for the parcels. To a large bowl, add the grated sweet potato, the chopped red onion, cannellini beans, the crushed garlic, crumbled feta, mint, and season with the salt and black pepper. Mix this round to combine, being careful not to squish it too much.

Then get the filo pastry out and ready, laid under a damp and clean tea towel, together with the rapeseed oil and a pastry brush.

You're going to make individual parcels, i.e. four of them. To make each parcel, lay out 3 sheets of pastry, one oblong on top of another. Use the rapeseed oil to brush all over each one, then put ¼ of the sweet potato mixture from the bowl near to one end of the oblongs, with 2cm space on either side of it. Fold the end of the oblong with the mixture on it inwards. Then fold in the sides in, and continue to fold the mixture so that you have created a parcel where the filling is entirely encased in pastry.

Lay the parcel carefully on a baking tray. Repeat for the next three parcels.

Put the baking tray with the parcels on top into an oven at 180° C / 350° F / Gas mark 4, and bake for 35 minutes, by which time the pastry will be cooked through and golden, and the filling will also be cooked.

While they are cooking, make the salad, and put it all in a suitable bowl.

Whisk the dressing ingredients together.

To serve, take the baking sheet out of the oven, and plate up the parcels. Immediately before serving pour the dressing over the salad and toss.

Lauren and I both hope you enjoy!

LIFE FOOD

Puy lentil, feta, and red pepper filo pie

Puy lentils are thought to be the best lentils. They are small, a kind of grey-green colour with a slightly mottled pattern on them. They hold their shape well, and have a sort of peppery flavour which is interestingly pleasant. "Puy" lentils have a protected Designation of Origin, and so they have to come from a specific place in the Auvergne region in France to qualify for the name. And the lentils are special. However, they're hard to source. As a result, when you're buying this kind of lentil in a supermarket you are almost certainly going to be buying "lentilles vertes" which are similar but not grown in the specific place.

It's nice to use this kind of lentil when the lentil is kind of pride of place in the meal. This recipe doesn't have many ingredients, but it delivers unique character, and evokes a sunny southern France kind of feel.

Serve with a lovely large leaf salad, maybe scattered with some toasted nuts.

Serves 4

Ingredients

Olive oil
3 cloves garlic, minced
2 teaspoons thyme, chopped finely
3 large red peppers
300g Puy lentils / lentilles vertes (dry weight)
900mls stock (vegetable or chicken), hot
Tomato puree
200g black olives, sliced
200g pack feta cheese
3 sheets of filo pastry
About 60ml combined of sunflower oil and melted butter

THE ABLE DIABETIC

Method

In a medium saucepan, warm some olive oil and lightly sauté the garlic and thyme for a minute. Add the stock, and then stir in the lentils, and the tomato puree. Get the pan to a low simmer and cook for 10 minutes.

Meanwhile, prepare the red peppers by deseeding them, and cutting out any internal membrane, then cut into large chunks. At the point the lentils have been cooking for 10 minutes, add them to the pan, and continue to cook for another 15 minutes. At this point, the lentils should be tender and cooked through. You want them just to have reached that point. There also shouldn't be much excess stock in the pan. If there is carefully spoon it off. Bring the pan off the heat and let it stand.

When it has cooled somewhat, stir through the black olives. Cut the block of feta into chunks and stir through too. Keep the chunks 1cm cubed or larger so that they survive being combined with the lentils as chunks.

Spoon the lentil mixture into an ovenproof dish that's about 18cm square.

To do the filo pastry topping, get the filo out of its box carefully. You only need 3 sheets so unfold it all, take three sheets off, and immediately wrap the remainder up, and put back in its packaging and back to the fridge. This recipe calls for much less care with the filo than is usual, and as long as you crack on with brushing the oil and melted butter mixture over the sheets and then crumpling them up a bit and laying them on top of the lentil mixture, you'll be fine. The objective is to cover the whole of the mixture evenly, but in a scrunched up way, to give lots of texture.

N.B. If you do want advice on handling the filo pastry, there are detailed instructions on how to use it in the recipe for Salmon and Broccoli filo quiche, so read that if you're not confident.

LIFE FOOD

The pie is ready to go into the oven now. Preheat the oven to 180° C / 350° F / Gas mark 4, and pop the dish in. The lentils are already cooked, so you are only heating it up fully, and cooking the top at this point, which will take about 30 minutes. The filo should be golden.

Serve the pie with a leafy salad and a nice dressing with a bit of sharpness to it which will complement the rich earthiness of the pie.

Beef and black bean noodles

Beef makes a rare appearance at my table, not because I don't love it, I do. It's because I am acutely aware of the environmental impact of farming beef, and I think it's a good policy to still eat it, but on select occasions, to buy high quality beef, and to treat it as a special thing. Which I really think it is.

My son, in his mid-teens, doesn't love my policy! He would eat steak every day if I put it in front of him. So, it seems only fair that I should include one of his favourites here. He loves this dish.

I love it too. And I love that this meal, because of the quite decent amount of broccoli that goes into it, balances out the carbs from the noodles. As it happens I made this last night, my blood sugars were about 8 before the meal, and I got something right because they didn't go above 10 afterwards and were steady all night. That's a recommendation if I ever made one!

Serves 4

Ingredients
Glug of sunflower oil
1 red onion, sliced
Lump of ginger root, peeled and minced
4 cloves garlic, minced
2 red birds' eye chillies, finely chopped
250g sirloin or rump steak – sliced into thin pieces
1 head of broccoli, chopped into bite sized pieces
1 red pepper, deseeded and chopped into bite sized pieces
Soy sauce
Sachet of black bean sauce
250g packet fine egg noodles
Sesame seeds to serve

LIFE FOOD

Method

Prepare everything before starting to cook: onion, garlic, ginger, and chilli, meat, and vegetables. Have them all to hand.

Before you start to cook the stir fry, get a pan of water to boil, and cook the noodles as per directions (3 minutes typically). Remove them and keep warm.

You will need a wide large wok-style or similar pan. Heat it to high on the hob, and be ready to add the ingredients quickly. Put the onion in, and briefly cook, then add the beef, garlic, ginger, diced chilli, and stir it around.

After a minute, add the broccoli and red pepper, and a dash of water, and put a lid over the pan to steam. This is a bit unorthodox by the way, but it works! Watch it carefully as you will need to stir quite frequently, but you do want the effect of the steam as well as the base heat. Once the broccoli is tender, reduce the heat to low, add the drained noodles, black bean sauce, and a good dash of the soy sauce, and stir to combine.

Serve in a large dish, with the sesame seeds sprinkled over, for people to help themselves. Soy sauce is very salty but my family like to add even more.

THE ABLE DIABETIC

Roast aubergines, chickpea mash and harissa

30 years ago, one of my favourite books, by one of my absolute favourite food writers, Nigel Slater, was gifted to me. Real Fast Food. It was a humble little tome, paperback, no photos, just full of brilliant recipes and joie de vivre. I'm emotionally attached to my somewhat battered copy. This recipe comes from there, and I don't think I've done much to make it my own, although the recipe below is what I do, so it's not word for word. But full credit to Nigel, a kitchen god.

I truly love aubergines too. Exotic, rich, and interesting, they bring something unique to meals, one of the few ingredients that don't have equivalent substitutes in my opinion.

This was one of the earliest times I came across the concept of combining potato with a pulse to make mash, and while these days pulse mashes are a common feature of trendy food, back then it was a real innovation. It is a healthy thing for anyone, bringing the protein value, the fibre and the lower carb content than straight potato, but especially for a t1d.

Serves 4

Ingredients

3 aubergines
3 cloves garlic
80ml extra virgin olive oil
2 large potatoes (300g in total)
2 cloves garlic
1 400g tin chickpeas, drained and rinsed
Salt
60ml Greek yogurt
Harissa (my favourite is Belazu rose harissa)
More olive oil

LIFE FOOD

Method

Start by washing the aubergines and cutting off their stalk. Cut each one lengthways, into half and then half again, and score the flesh deeply with a knife. You want the aubergine to stay whole, but the cutting allows the heat and garlic to penetrate more deeply. Put the aubergine pieces on a baking tray. Take the first 3 cloves of garlic and remove the papery skins, then slice the cloves thinly and poke the slivers into the aubergine wedges. Drizzle the olive oil over the aubergine.

Pop the baking tray into a hot oven, 180° C / 350° F / Gas mark 4, and roast for 30 minutes, by which time the wedges should be starting to char around the edges and if you poke a sharp knife into one it will give no resistance.

Meanwhile, make the mash. Peel the potatoes, and chop into chunks. Also peel the two remaining garlic cloves and pop both potatoes and garlic into a medium saucepan with some water and boil / steam them until the potato chunks are tender and ready to mash. Add the drained chickpeas at this point and warm them through – this will only take a couple of minutes. Drain the potatoes and chickpeas, add a good couple of dollops of Greek yogurt, and a good pinch of salt and mash until smooth. The texture will be different to pure potato mash, and that's how you want it, with just a bit more natural nuttiness.

The last thing to prep is the harissa drizzle, by taking a good couple of heaped teaspoons of harissa and loosening with some more olive oil so it is quite runny.

To serve, put a big blob of the mash onto warmed plates, and arrange the wedges on top. Then drizzle (or let people do this themselves) over the harissa-y olive oil.

I relish this meal with nothing else, but some roasted tomatoes, and maybe a baby spinach salad would be nice.

THE ABLE DIABETIC

Seared tuna, cannellini mash, roast tomatoes and olives

I'm feeling apologetic for not including more fish recipes in this book. It's not that we don't eat fish, we just tend to eat the recipes with mackerel over and over again.

This recipe is therefore a real treat. Please buy tuna that is Marine Stewardship Council approved.

The tuna goes so well with the beautiful cannellini mash, and the tomatoes bring sweetness and wonderful colour. This is a fabulous meal which is perfect for a t1d.

Serves 4

Ingredients

Glug of olive oil
4 pieces of tuna, each 180-200g
1 large lemon, juiced
4 large tomatoes
2 cloves garlic
2 400g tins cannellini beans
100g black olives preferably in oil
Salt and black pepper

Method

Start by putting the tuna on a plate. Mix the juice of the lemon and a good glug of olive oil together and pour over the tuna. Let it marinate for 30 minutes. While it's doing that you can do the rest of the meal preparation and cooking.

Next, get the tomatoes ready for roasting. Cut each one in half along its middle (the equator) and place all the halves in a suitable roasting dish. Take the papery skin off the garlic cloves and then slice the garlic and poke the slices evenly into all the tomatoes. Drizzle olive oil over them and pop them in the oven at 180° C / 350° F / Gas mark 4. They'll take 30 minutes.

Slice the black olives and set aside.

While they are cooking, make the cannellini mash by draining and rinsing the beans and putting them in a saucepan with just a small amount of water – enough to keep them from sticking to the bottom. Gently warm them up, and when they're hot, stir in a glug of olive oil and mash them until smooth. Keep warm.

You should cook the tuna immediately before serving people. When you're ready, heat up a griddle pan that will fit all the tuna pieces, and get it hot. Add the tuna to the griddle pan and cook without moving them for 2-3 minutes. Then turn over, and cook for a further 2 minutes. This will give you tuna that is 'medium', cooked on the outside but still pink in the middle. Cooking tuna is like cooking steak: people's preferences range from rare to well done. So, adapt the cooking time to meet what people enjoy. That said, it's a shame to serve quality tuna and for it to be overdone.

To serve, place a quarter of the mash on each plate with 2 half tomatoes alongside, the olive slices sprinkled over, and the tuna next to or on top of the mash. Let people add their own salt and black pepper.

SALADS

SALADS

Tabbouleh

Fattoush

Carrot and nut salad

(Nigella's) noodle salad

Waldorf salad

Coleslaw

Butternut squash and feta salad

Beetroot and goats' cheese salad

Griddled asparagus, pear and goats' cheese salad

LIFE FOOD

I have a view that there is more scope for a salad to be either amazing or disappointing, than for other kinds of meals. I know that's a debatable view, and as an example, being faced with a soup that's like dishwater is pretty grim. But it seems the spectrum is wider for salads to me.

And maybe that's why as a proportion of what I've eaten in my life, salads are a relatively small part, even though I would always have said I like them. What I mean is I like the good ones. A salad can be vivacious, enlivening, thoroughly joyful when it is got right.

Salad does take a decent amount of preparation though. There seems to be more chopping, slicing, grating, arranging than with other kinds of food prep. It's hard to short cut these tasks. And a busy life doesn't always accommodate them.

With the family, and if the salad is the main meal, in my experience the challenge is to make it sufficiently hearty and sustaining. I'm not going to gloss over the fact that my boys would generally rather have a lasagne / shepherd's pie / roast / insert solid meal here, than a salad. The reality is therefore that either I serve the salad with generous and carb-laden sides such as rice or bread, or I build a lot into the salad. And I do both. Many of my recipes here, including tabbouleh and the noodle salad, have substantial underpinning!

Another note I'd make is that I am a great believer, especially when you have a larger group of family and friends, in having food which is 'build your own' plate. Lots of people have reasons for not wanting to eat certain foods. Tapas or mezze style food is great. I would always include a salad in this kind of spread. I'd also include some of the things I write about in the Lighter Meals section. As a tld, I'd love to be offered a range of food that included salad, roasted vegetables, and a borek.

Getting back to salads, they occupy a higher proportion of my food than they used to. I have learnt ways, such as using cans or jars of beans and lentils, that make preparation quicker. I buy things that are easy to use. Straightforward ingredients like carrots and courgettes are added as ribbons, or grated, for speed and ease.

The bottom line, talking about me as a t1d, is that a well-constructed salad, starting with a good bed of lettuce or spinach leaves, with some other vegetables chopped and layered over, maybe a sprinkling of rice and grains, some nuts, then cheese, smoked fish, or boiled eggs, and a good dressing, is a wonderful and beautifully balanced meal. The ratios of veg to carb to protein is easy to get right. Eating a meal like this truly ticks the t1d box. And so, I definitely encourage it. Salads definitely have their place in my life.

I hope what I offer here covers both some of those more family friendly options and also meal-salads that deliver on the amazing promise a great salad has. Check out the pear and asparagus one!

LIFE FOOD

THE ABLE DIABETIC

Tabbouleh

If I had to choose one cuisine to eat for the rest of my life it would be Lebanese.

When I make tabbouleh I always remember one that came from the food hall at Harrods. My youngest brother was vegan and, long before vegan food was mainstream, in the search for lunch for him, this was where we ended up. It was sublime.

This is a wonderful food to make for a t1d because it has so much freshness, fibre and vegetable goodness, with the carbs, coming from a wholegrain, very much playing a minor and supporting role. Everything about this is good. I must admit that I don't use bulgur wheat for anything else, and I only buy it occasionally when this recipe comes to mind. It's worth buying though, and I find over a summer, we can easily get through a 500g bag of bulgur wheat.

Ingredients
100g bulgur wheat, washed
1 large bunch fresh flat leaved parsley
1 large bunch mint
2 large lemons
3 cloves garlic, minced
1 large cucumber
4 large, ripe tomatoes
1 red onion
Generous glug extra virgin olive oil

Method

The first job is to cook the bulgur wheat. Bring 500ml of water to boil in a small saucepan and add the grains. Cover the pan with a lid, put the heat on low-medium to get to a gentle simmer, and simmer for 12-15 minutes. Take off the heat and let it stand for a further 10 minutes. If there is any residual water, drain it off. Let the bulgur wheat cool down completely.

THE ABLE DIABETIC

While that is going on, get a large bowl and prep the other ingredients. The key thing here is that everything needs to be cut super small, to dice of about ½ cm. Start with the cucumber, and remove the central soft seedy part before dicing. For the tomatoes, I retain the seeds, but some people will prefer them being removed. Whether you do that or not, cut the tomatoes small. Dice the red onion finely.

When it comes to the herbs, the more you use, the better. I have a terrible habit of thinking that I'll save a bit of the bunches for something else, but since sometimes they don't get used, far better to use them all here! Wash the herbs well and trim off the ends of the stalk. That's the only part you should discard. For the rest of both herbs, chop them finely, stalks and all, and put the whole pile into the bowl.

Peel the garlic cloves and crush them. Add to the bowl.

When the bulgur wheat is cold, add it to the chopped salad and herbs. Then pour over the olive oil, and the juice of the lemons.

Eat as soon as you can.

Fattoush

A large, chopped salad is a great lunch option. This has been a favourite of mine for many years. It has real zing.

The three things that are essential in this salad are the radishes, the lemon and the Sumac. Together they give the salad loads of pep. Sumac is a Middle Eastern spice which has a lemony, slightly sharp taste. This is a lively bowlful.

The only carb in this salad is the pitta bread. One pitta of about 60g in weight provides 30g of carb, so this recipe split 4 ways gives a portion size of 15g carb. The right kind of lunch amount for me.

Serves 4

Ingredients
2 pitta bread (white or wholemeal)
1 cucumber
300g punnet of cherry tomatoes
1 red onion
250g radishes
1 head Romaine lettuce
1 bunch of mint
1 bunch of parsley
1-2 teaspoons sumac
1 tablespoon extra-virgin olive oil
2 lemons
1 clove garlic, minced
Salt & black pepper

Method

Get a large salad bowl ready.

Start by breaking the pitta bread into small torn pieces, about 1-2cm in size and scatter all over a baking sheet. Put this into a medium hot oven, 160° C / 325° F / Gas mark 3, and cook until toasted and golden brown. Take out and allow to cool completely. You can do this well ahead.

Prepare the salad by deseeding the cucumber and chopping, halving the cherry tomatoes, slicing the radishes, slicing the red onion into smallish pieces, and washing and shredding the Romaine lettuce. Put all of those ingredients in the salad bowl.

Wash the mint and parsley well. Pull the mint leaves off their stalks, and chop quite finely. Finely chop the parsley stalks and leaves. Put all the herbs into the bowl. Sprinkle over the sumac.

Make the dressing by combining the lemon juice, olive oil, minced garlic, salt and pepper, and whisking well to combine.

When you're ready to serve, sprinkle the toasted pitta over the salad, and pour over the dressing. Toss well and serve immediately.

LIFE FOOD

Carrot and nut salad

I like having this salad in the repertoire because I almost never don't have carrots in the house, and it is cheap and easy. I know this isn't a standalone salad, but it can be perfect for those moments when you seem to have nothing fresh around, and yet you want something that will work for a healthy lunch.

It also often features in a selection of salads that we would have for a meal.

Recipes that are cheap, effective and don't involve a trip to the shops do have a special place in my heart. Let's not forget either that carrots are an underrated superfood - very good for you.

Serves 4 as part of a meal

Ingredients

800g carrots
200g of nuts: walnuts, hazelnuts preferred
1 lemon, juiced
2 tablespoons walnut oil (or sunflower or rapeseed)
Salt and black pepper
1 grated apple
75g raisins

Method

Peel and top and tail the carrots. I would wash them after I've done this as well. Then grate the carrots using the coarse side of a grater straight into a bowl.

Chop the nuts up, not too finely, and add them to the carrots. Grate or chop the apple into small pieces. Personally, I prefer chopped. Sprinkle the apple and the raisins into the bowl.

THE ABLE DIABETIC

Whisk together the lemon juice, oil, and a little salt and pepper, and pour over the ingredients in the bowl. Toss well. You're done! It's all ready to eat.

(Nigella's) noodle salad

Hilariously, Nigella says of her recipe, "I always make a large vat of these noodles since they're lovely to pick at in the fridge."! It's true: they are very hard to resist! I offer them here as a legitimate lunch not as an ever-present grazing facility!

I'm staying fairly close to the original recipe here, but I have increased the amount of veg, to make the carb to veg ratio better for me.

The original recipe also includes mangetouts which I don't buy if they've been air freighted. The best alternative I've found is good old English broccoli, which does add a bit of work because it needs a little bit of cooking. I think the effort is worth it.

Ingredients

250g of dried egg noodles
125g mangetout or head of broccoli cut into small florets
150g beansprouts
2 red peppers
5 spring onions
Sprinkle of sesame seeds, about 50g
Bunch of coriander

Dressing:
1 tablespoon sesame oil
1 tablespoon garlic infused oil or olive oil and some crushed garlic
1 tablespoon soy sauce
2 tablespoon sweet chilli sauce
100g chunky peanut butter
2 tablespoons fresh lime juice

THE ABLE DIABETIC

<u>Method</u>

Start by cooking the noodles, according to the packet instructions. Let them cool.

Deseed and then chop the red peppers into quite small pieces, suitable for eating with a fork, and slice the spring onions into small dice. Cut the broccoli into small, again forkable, florets, and cook briefly in some boiling water, for just 2-3 minutes, and then run cold water over them so they are still firm and vibrantly green. Combine all these vegetables in a large bowl, together with the bean sprouts. N.B. if you are using mangetout, they just need slicing up.

Prepare the coriander. Wash it, then take the leaves off the stalks, reserve them, and chop the stalks up small.

Make the dressing by whisking all the oils and sauces in the dressing ingredients together in a bowl.

Add the noodles to the vegetables in the bowl. Pour over the dressing and mix everything up well. Then add the coriander and turn over to combine. Sprinkle with the sesame seeds.

Makes a fab packed lunch.

LIFE FOOD

Waldorf salad

I find those supermarket tubs of gloopy salads depressing. Some are particularly far from a proper version of themselves, and top of the pile in my view is Waldorf. Although I've noticed that these days they're called 'apple, celery and walnut' salad. I like knowing that it was invented somewhere, and has a history, its own character. The name does mean something! There's also a humorous episode of Fawlty Towers that Waldorf salad features in. I am getting all historical now.

The way I make it, there is quite a lot of the three main ingredients - celery, apples, walnuts – with a small quantity of grapes and a lighter dressing than the original. I like it light and crisp, so fresh celery and crisp apple is the way to go.

Although I like mayonnaise, and it is in our fridge, it doesn't turn up much either in our food or on our table. Sometimes it is worth the calories and the fat – for me this is one of those times.

When you look at this recipe in its entirety, it delivers a lot of benefits and is far from unhealthy.

Ingredients

5 generous sticks of celery
1 crisp apple
100g walnuts
10 grapes – can be green or black: seedless
Juice from ½ a large lemon
1 tablespoon Greek yogurt
½ tablespoon mayonnaise (Hellman's in our house)

Method

This is just a chop and assemble job!

THE ABLE DIABETIC

Wash the celery, and top and tail. If the celery stalks are extra-broad, cut them in half lengthwise, but generally, just cut into small pieces all the way along the length. I aim for slices about 2-3mm thick. Pop into a large bowl.

Core the apple, and chop into smallish chunks, then pop them into the bowl. No need to peel. The skin is good for you.

At this point, squeeze the lemon juice all over the apple and celery.

Next chop the walnut into fairly small pieces. Not crumbled, but not chunky.

Quarter your grapes and throw them in.

Blend the Greek yogurt and mayonnaise in a separate bowl and then add to the main bowl and stir everything to coat it. It should be a light coating, so that the main ingredients sing.

LIFE FOOD

Coleslaw

I know coleslaw is only coleslaw but bear with me.

My love of coleslaw goes back to 1990-91 when I was at school in the USA. It was something that you'd see in the UK, even back then, when it would be a drippy and damp concoction. In the USA though, it was so much better. Social cookouts were a big part of USA life, and coleslaw cropped up a lot. I loved their crunchy, yet rich salad.

When I was older and decided to make it myself, the things that came home to me clearly were (wow) how incredibly cheap and (wow) how incredibly easy! Since that realisation, when I have bought a supermarket pot the voice is my head is screaming "a waste of money, Sarah, AND more plastic". In the last decade the plastic argument has won. I don't buy, I make. It seems so bad to deliver a little plastic box to landfill for a few forkfuls of cabbage and carrot.

Coleslaw can be adapted easily. The basic recipe is straightforward and perfectly good. If you want to ring the changes, easy. More often than not, ours has the mayo lightened with yogurt.

My children aren't keen on mayonnaise. So, often instead of the cabbage and carrots being dressed in mayo, I go instead with a dressing made of sunflower oil, diced red chillies, and a bit of rice vinegar. It's slightly oriental, and they much prefer it.

Coleslaw is obviously always served with something else. As part of a salad. Possibly in a sandwich with some cheese. Maybe if I'm having a baked potato. It's a low stress addition to a meal because it's low in carbs and contains lots of fibre.

Overall, coleslaw is easy going, overdelivers and deserves to appear on the table.

Serve as part of a larger meal.

THE ABLE DIABETIC

<u>Ingredients</u>
2 medium carrots
¼ white cabbage
1 tablespoon mayonnaise

And if you want to, additions:
Some spring onions or ½ red onion or chives
30g good mature grated cheddar
Sour cream or crème fraiche in place of some of the mayo

<u>Method</u>

You need a largish bowl for the preparation (which is a bit messy), and a different serving bowl.

Start by washing then shredding the cabbage, and putting it in the prep bowl. Peel, top and tail the carrots, and then coarsely grate them into the bowl too. If you're going to add the onions or cheddar, do that now.

Add the mayonnaise (or mayo/yogurt mix) and stir into the cabbage and carrots.

Transfer to the serving bowl and chill until ready to eat (this keeps well).

LIFE FOOD

Butternut squash and feta salad

Lauren loves this salad, so for that reason, and because it's a great balanced meal for me, it deserves inclusion in this book.

Butternut is a gorgeous vegetable that does have carbs in it, but also holds its own as a main ingredient. All up this salad contains about 15g of carb per portion.

If you want to make the salad more substantial, it will happily take a bit of cold brown rice sprinkled over it, or some cooked puy style lentils. Obviously that adds carbs, but it's a choice for you.

You can serve this as a hot salad, with the butternut straight out of the oven. I like it when the butternut has cooled a bit but is still warm. I like how it works with the cheese, slightly melding, but not so much as to make everything slick. Likewise, if you wanted the whole thing prepped ahead and served cold, that's totally doable.

We treat bacon as a treat. Here, a couple of bacon rashers, chopped into small pieces, grilled to crispy, and crumbled over this is delicious.

Serves 4

Ingredients

Salad leaves (any kind you want), about 200g in total
Half a butternut squash (about 500g weight of prepared flesh)
Glug of sunflower oil
The butternut seeds, washed
100g walnuts
200g feta cheese
50 ml walnut oil / olive oil
25 ml white wine vinegar
1 teaspoon Dijon mustard

THE ABLE DIABETIC

Salt & black pepper

Method

This salad benefits from being served in a fairly low, wide, flat bowl or platter. But any that fits are fine.

Start with the butternut squash preparation. Peel off the skin, taking care to minimise waste. (Some people would happily eat the skin, but it's not my choice). Scoop out the seeds from the middle of the squash and separate the seeds from the membrane and stringy stuff. Wash the seeds, then dry and put, spread out, on a baking tray, and cover entirely with foil. Put the baking tray in a hot oven, 180° C / 350° F / Gas mark 4, for 10 minutes to toast the seeds (this can be done alongside the butternut chunks that we're just coming to). Remove and cool.

Cut the squash flesh into bite sized pieces, 1-2cm cube style. Put the chunks on a baking tray that has a small amount of sunflower oil on it and then into the oven. Roast for 40 minutes, or until the chunks are cooked through and browned. Set aside, leaving on the tray.

While the butternut is cooking do the other preparation. Chop the walnuts up into small pieces. Crumble the feta cheese into small pieces. Prepare the dressing by whisking the oil, wine vinegar, Dijon mustard, salt and pepper.

Assemble the salad by sprinkling the feta, walnuts, and seeds over the leaves. You can do all this before the final stage when you add the butternut.

When you are ready to eat, and the butternut is out of the oven and at whatever temperature you prefer, spoon the chunks evenly over the whole salad. Then drizzle the dressing across the entire salad, also evenly.

LIFE FOOD

Beetroot and goats' cheese salad

One of the lovely things about your children getting older is that suddenly they think beetroot, previously completely disgusting, is "delicious", and a whole new set of meals comes into view. Another thing that both my children did was arrive at a point where salad was a requested food. Miracles do happen!

Lauren doesn't get on easily with cows' milk, so goats' cheese has played a significant role in our diets for a long time. It's delicious, and its tangy freshness complements and cuts through the sweet earthy richness of beetroot beautifully.

This salad is relatively low carb, with the beetroot itself having some, the lentils adding protein, fibre, and some carbs, and the croutons also counting. I would need a fairly low measure of insulin with the salad as it stands, and would likely add an additional small bread roll or slice of bread if this was a main meal. I like having meals at my fingertips that do come in needing less insulin though, and this is substantial enough without lots of carbs. We all think this salad is a winner.

Serves 4

Ingredients

Glug sunflower oil
400g baby spinach, washed well
100g puy style dried lentils
450g uncooked beetroot or 350g cooked beetroot
100-200g soft goats' cheese
100g walnuts
1-2 slices seedy bread
50ml walnut oil
25ml lemon juice, preferably freshly squeezed
1 teaspoon wholegrain mustard
Salt & black pepper – a good pinch

THE ABLE DIABETIC

<u>Method</u>

If you're using raw beetroot, which is my preference, because I like this served warm, peel the beetroot, cut into chunks, lightly dribbled with sunflower oil, and put on baking tray, then into an oven to roast for 30m until tender. I would leave it sat in the cooling oven until ready to assemble.

Also deal with the bread which is to become croutons. Cut or tear into bite sized pieces, and sprinkle with a small amount of olive oil, then put on a baking tray. Close to the end of the beetroot cooking time, put the baking tray into the same oven and cook for 5-8 minutes until browned and crispy. Set aside.

In parallel, cook the lentils, by simmering for the time recommended, about 20-30 minutes. Once cooked, drain.

Cut the goats' cheese into small pieces and set aside.

Chop the walnuts into pieces, just under a centimetre big.

To make the dressing, combine the walnut oil, lemon juice, wholegrain mustard, and salt and pepper and whisk well. (By the way, using lemon juice means that its vitamin C helps your body access the iron in the spinach, which is an important nutritional component. For the same reason, this salad can have orange segments added to it, which both tastes great, and is super healthy).

It's now time to assemble the salad. If you are using warm beetroot, do this quickly, and get to the table quickly too, because the heat will wilt the spinach, which is lovely, but you don't want to let it go too far. Start with a bed of spinach leaves, sprinkle the puy lentils over, then the goats' cheese, and walnuts. Add the beetroot, and then the croutons, and drizzle with the dressing.

Serve immediately.

Griddled asparagus, pear and goats' cheese salad

This recipe has its roots in time spent with friends in the south of France when I was in my late 20s. Nathalie was an amazing cook, and she presented a super-luxe version of this with champagne vinegar specially sourced. I've slightly simplified it for day to day enjoyment in our home, and it is wow delicious. A treat in the asparagus season.

This is a low carb meal. The pears contribute some carbs, but overall, this is low. Eating this requires a small dose of insulin. It is helpful to have this in my repertoire, because it can, for example, be followed by a light pasta, or some kind of dessert without requiring extra insulin. As such, it has a special and useful place in my world. Without being part of a multi-course meal, I would likely have a bread roll on the side.

Serves 4

Ingredients

Mixed leaves, including spinach, lambs' lettuce, and English lettuce – a fairly soft selection
A little sunflower oil
2 firm pears
Bunch asparagus
200g goats' cheese
50 ml extra virgin olive oil
20ml white wine vinegar
1 teaspoon wholegrain mustard

Method

There are three aspects to making this meal. The first is prepping the salad base which is straightforward, involving laying out the leaves (obviously washed, spun, and picked through) and crumbling the goats' cheese and sprinkling over the lettuce.

The second is prepping the dressing, which just involves whisking together the olive oil, white wine vinegar, and wholegrain mustard.

The main event is the griddling. First, prep the asparagus, cutting off the woody part of the stems. For the pears, wash, quarter, cut out the cores, and slice each quarter into 2-3 slices.

You'll need a large griddle pan for this, and if you don't have a large one, cook the asparagus first and keep it warm. If possible, cook the asparagus and pear at the same time. Lightly grease the griddle with sunflower oil, and lay out the asparagus and pear slices on it. Heat the griddle and leave them in place for several minutes before moving to create spots on the veg and fruit that are browned, and in the case of the pears slightly caramelised. Turn over when half-cooked, and continue to griddle until both the asparagus and pear are tender and cooked through.

Take off the heat and immediately lay on the prepared salad leaves, and pour the dressing on over all elements.

LIGHTER MEALS

LIGHTER MEALS

Peppered mackerel pâté

Roasted peppers

Stuffed mushrooms

Vietnamese rice wraps

Mediterranean chicken borek

Chickpeas with Indian-spiced stir-fried greens

Butternut and red lentil pâté

Spanish tortilla

Provençale mixed lentils and grains

LIFE FOOD

As I was writing this book I realised that I have a few things I turn to that don't qualify as full meals but are still undoubtedly useful to me. They're things I might make for myself, rather than a group, or they'd be served as part of some kind of a buffet-style meal, or as a simple meal with a friend who comes for lunch. They aren't necessarily a meal in themselves, and they get used in different ways; they're extra! Whatever the label is, they deserve a place because they crop up a lot. It would be odd, and wrong, to leave them out.

Like many people, I would turn to a ham or cheese sandwich when I'm looking for a simple, quick and unfussy light meal, and that leads to both eating too much bread, and a high calorie meal with limited other nutrition. I hope this chapter offers you alternatives which are both not boring and are also healthy.

In our house, the most common way these crop up is for a lunch or supper when for some reason we're not all together. Many of them do need an accompaniment, which could be bread, crackers, or crudites. They might be served with a salad too.

They are generally either non-carb or low carb. You might choose to eat some with bread or toast. Some are quite high fat, so while not a 'full meal' should be balanced with something vegetable based. Using ingredients like filo pastry and rice paper wrappers gives structure combined with low carb impact.

I think missing them out would have been an oversight. I hope including them helps to tip the balance towards interesting, varied, and different.

THE ABLE DIABETIC

LIFE FOOD

Peppered mackerel pâté

I'm pretty sure this was introduced to me by my friend Nicola when we were in our twenties. I don't see anything like as much as I'd like to see of her these days but she's one of those people whose friendship matters. And the mackerel pâté is a bonus.

I've said before that mackerel is a central foodstuff in our home, and we eat it more smoked than any other way. I love it, and I love that I love something which is basically all good!

Smoked mackerel is fantastic in this recipe because it has a powerful flavour. Pâté works best when it packs a punch. You don't need tonnes of it to feel you've eaten well, and it makes a simple meal readily satisfying.

This is ridiculously easy to make. Anyone, with basic tools, can make it. It's literally a 5 minute job. I buy smoked mackerel once a week and so we always have it in the fridge. It lasts well unopened, so I recommend it as a generally useful ingredient to have to hand.

The pâté suits toast, crackers, and sits well on slices of cucumber, celery sticks, and sliced up raw carrot. I think it likes something pickled like cornichons or baby pickled onions on the side too. It makes a perfect lunch option for a t1d. A little pâté, a slice of seedy wholesome toast, and a little pile of cucumber, celery, carrot. Brilliantly enjoyable and all the right components.

Serves 4 generously

Ingredients

200g of smoked, peppered mackerel
100g cream cheese (such as Philadelphia)
½ lemon, juiced
More freshly ground black pepper

THE ABLE DIABETIC

Method

I use a stick blender to make this, but I've used a food processor and have also made it by hand with a fork.

Flake the mackerel into whatever receptacle you're using. Add the cream cheese and lemon juice. Pulse, whiz or mash until it is smooth (or as smooth as you want it). Hand mashing with not get it to a perfectly smooth consistency but that doesn't stop it from being perfect.

Decant into a suitable dish and sprinkle the extra ground pepper over the top.

You should refrigerate the pâté if you're not eating it soon. It'll last a couple of days covered in the fridge, but I'd be surprised if it does!

Roasted peppers

I was a fairly new t1d, in my mid-twenties, when I found this recipe, and it has been made more times than I could possibly count, and has proved hugely useful. It goes without saying that it is a deeply flavoursome, vibrant dish, which brings brightness into any day. I never don't love it.

The reason it has proved so useful is that it is so flexible. It can be a starter, a part of a buffet, a main course with sides. It can be served on its own, on salad leaves, or on top of a piece of toasted ciabatta, bruschetta-style. It can be served hot, warm, or cold.

I often include it in a set of different salad style things in the summer, alongside salamis, cheese, crudites. Whether I serve it on bread or not depends on what else is going on. In this way, I am enabled to manage the carb-load of a meal, and the insulin I need.

Unless as part of a spread, I would give 1 pepper per person, so they get 2 halves of a pepper on their plate. The way of serving here is with the peppers on ciabatta so there are carbs built in. However, if you want to reduce or eradicate the bread, do, and serve the peppers on salad leaves.

Serves 4

Ingredients

4 red and / or yellow peppers
6 medium sized ripe tomatoes
3 cloves garlic
Generous glug of extra virgin olive oil
8 anchovies
8 black olives

4 ciabatta rolls or 1 large ciabatta loaf

THE ABLE DIABETIC

<u>Method</u>

For this you need a large baking dish or tray with a lip around the edge which will accommodate the 8 pepper halves and contain juices.

Preheat the oven to 160° C / 325° F / Gas mark 3.

Start by cutting each of the peppers in half, slicing through the stalks so that each half retains theirs. Then carefully cut out the white pith, and the seeds, but leave the stalk intact. You should have clean looking pepper 'boats'. Try not to put your knife through the pepper flesh at any point because the juices that emerge during cooking will leak out. Lay the pepper halves on the baking tray.

Cut each of the tomatoes into quarters, and place 3 quarters in each pepper 'boat'.

Take the paper off each of the garlic cloves, and slice the garlic thinly. Push the garlic slices into the tomatoes, distributing them across the 8 pepper boats evenly.

Put a small glug of olive oil into each pepper boat. Then slice the black olives into halves lengthways, and lay the 2 olive halves and an anchovy on each pepper. By the way, if you have anyone who doesn't eat fish, or anyone who might want something a little less punchy, you can omit the olives and anchovies from some or all of the peppers.

The peppers then go into the oven where they will roast for 45 minutes, or until they look toasty and cooked. This is a flexible and easy meal – if you want the peppers to cook more slowly, turn the oven down, or just leave them in the oven once you've turned it off. And if you're in a rush, a hotter oven will work more quickly and won't create any disasters!

LIFE FOOD

As you're cooking the peppers, cook the ciabatta so it is toasted too i.e. by slicing it through the middle, and serve by laying the peppers on a piece of bread so that any juice trickles into it.

Food of the gods.

Stuffed mushrooms

When I was in my early thirties, newly living in southwest London, a real joy in life was that my lovely second cousin, Sonya, lived not far away, and we used to see each other regularly. Having good people in your life is one of the greatest blessings, and Sonya is good through and through. The best. I love her to bits. Sonya has been a vegetarian since she was in her teens. I loved her cooking for me (I think the first good dhal I ever ate was in her flat), and I loved cooking for her. This recipe takes me back to our chatty, funny, slightly crazy conversations as young women enjoying life. For some reason I recall her loving these stuffed mushrooms. They are fab: juicy, crunchy, richly flavoured. Someone once said that life is too short to stuff a mushroom, and this proves that to be rubbish! Sonya, this is for you.

I don't eat enough mushrooms because they're not popular at ours. A shame. I get that they are in a special class of their own as fungi, and I understand why some people find them too weird to eat. It's a shame because their uniqueness extends to their nutritional qualities. They are not like plants. They have lots of B vitamins, and are a rare natural food source of vitamin D. Additionally they contain other minerals and compounds that have a wide range of benefits. They are very low in carbohydrate.

This recipe includes some breadcrumbs for the stuffing, which translates into a quarter of a slice of bread per portion. If you want a nil-to-low carb meal, eat the mushrooms with salad. Or, if you're looking for something heavier, they go great on top of a slice of toast.

A stuffed mushroom is a substantial thing, and however served, is as delicious a dinner as you could want.

Serves 4

LIFE FOOD

Ingredients

4 substantial large mushrooms, portobello or similar
Wholemeal / other good brown bread, about 1 thick slice, made into breadcrumbs e.g. in a food processor / hand blender
4 cloves garlic, minced
50g butter - softened (or olive oil)
Any fresh herbs, my favourite are tarragon and thyme

Method

You'll need a dish or tray that can go into the oven with the four mushrooms lying flat, snugly.

Heat the oven to 170° C / 340° F / Gas mark 3. Preparation doesn't take long.

Wash and wipe the mushrooms. For each mushroom, neatly cut the stalk where it joins the cap so that when the mushroom is upside down it is level.

Take the stalks, and trim and discard the bottom bit (where it met the soil) then finely chop the stalk up. Mix the chopped stalk with the minced garlic, and the butter (or olive oil). Chop the herbs and add them and the breadcrumbs to the butter as well. Mix well.

Take a ¼ of the breadcrumb-butter mixture and press into the upturned mushroom cups, one by one. Get as much as you can in because as the mushrooms cook, their juice seeps into the breadcrumbs.

Place the mushrooms in the dish or tray and pop straight into the oven, and cook for 30 minutes. These are best when the stuffing has both absorbed all the mushroom juice, the garlic and herbs have thoroughly infused, and the topping has gone crunchy too.

Eat them hot from the oven.

Vietnamese rice wraps

Jim and I met in a bar in Bangkok in 2002. We were both backpacking around Asia. A month or so later we were in Vietnam where I first encountered the concept of "fresh" spring rolls. I had only known the fried ones before that and although they are nice as a rare treat, they are nothing like as good as these in my opinion. These are absolutely delicious and vibrant as well as being super light and healthy. Eventually, they've become common to see in London, but I still don't think of them as entirely mainstream. For Jim and me, they will always bring to mind fun times and happy memories.

The first time I tried to make these I did it with Jim as we were getting ready for friends coming over. We found the process quite a challenge! Wetting the rice paper sheets so they are malleable, and then rolling them neatly into small packages was hard and took practice. The first few were scrappy and falling apart. It was fun to learn, and as with so many things, the key to success was in the preparation.

The best tip to make the spring rolls delicious is to use lots of fresh mint and fresh coriander. And then to make the sauce tingling hot and salty. Zingy and fresh!

The note for a diabetic eater here is that rice wraps are a perfect way to keep the carb quotient of a meal in the low zone, while having plenty of fresh veg and protein. While these are designed to be eaten several in one portion as finger food, for a proper meal, you can size up the wrap and increase the filling. The ratio of filling to rice paper increases, so these are great as a light carb lunch.

Serves 4 (as a meal)

LIFE FOOD

<u>Ingredients</u>

Packet of rice paper wrappers – hard to say how many you'll need, especially factoring in breakage!
Filling:
1 large cucumber, washed and seeds removed
2-3 large carrots, peeled, top and bottom removed
300g cooked King prawns
Big bunch of mint
Big bunch of coriander
150g rice vermicelli noodles

Dipping sauce:
2 limes - juiced
A few dashes fish sauce
A little sugar
20ml Sunflower oil
1 garlic clove (minced)
8 Bird's eye chillies, red and green, finely chopped

Start with the prep of what you are going to fill the wrappers with. You are going to making long thin parcels, so cut the cucumber and carrots into super thin batons, only 2mm thick, and 5cm long.
Cut the prawns lengthways.

Wash the coriander well, then remove the leaves from the stems, pretty much into individual leaves. You can use the stems if you want, but you need to chop them into tiny dice that can be sprinkled.

Similarly wash the mint well and then pick off the leaves. I don't use the stems.

Cook the vermicelli noodles by putting them into boiling water for a few moments. They go soft quickly. As soon as they reach a point where they are not firm but movable, dunk them into cold water to stop them cooking further and then drain well. If you overcook them you'll end up with unworkable white sludge.

With those 5 things done, you're ready to move onto assembling the wraps themselves.

The wraps may come in different sizes. For small spring rolls you need either wraps of 20cm in diameter or wraps 30cm in diameter that you have cut into halves (semi-circle shapes). You need these ready.

Your workspace for the assembly stage is important. You will need space to be able to move through the stages quickly and cleanly. I like this in a kind of 'production line' style set up with the dry rice paper wrappers on the left, the bowl of hot water they are to be dipped in next to them, an open space that is big enough to lay the rice paper wrapper out in front of me, and the prepped filling ingredients in bowls to the right.

This enables the process as follows:

- Taking a dry rice paper wrapper, dip it into newly boiled hot water very gently and quickly, allowing it to get just to a point where it is flexible. If you leave the wrapper immersed too long it will disintegrate.
- Place the wrapper flat on the workspace and then lay a small pile of carrots and cucumber all in a neat bundle at one end of the wrapper.
- Then lay 1-2 sliced prawns on the carrot and cucumber.
- Sprinkle mint and coriander leaves over.
- Once done you need to fold the sides inward and roll the bundle lengthwise to make a spring roll shape. The wrappers will be just sticky enough to connect so that once you've done the roll, you can leave aside to 'settle'.
- Try to lay the spring rolls apart from each other while they dry out, and while you make the whole set.
- N.B., you can make these very pretty by laying the ingredients out nicely, especially the coriander leaves, as they will be visible once made through the transparent wrapper.

LIFE FOOD

The Nuoc cham dipping sauce to accompany is very easy. Put the wet ingredients (lime juice, sunflower oil, fish sauce) in a jar and add the sugar. Stir to dissolve. Then add the crushed garlic and finely chopped chillis. Stir well. Taste and adjust.. if it needs to be tangier a dash more fish sauce. It should be very spicy and impactful!

These can be chilled for a few hours until you want to eat them. They aren't nice if left to warm, and the prawns would go a bit gross quite quickly. Great eaten with friends.

Mediterranean chicken borek

At the time of King Charles' coronation in 2023 I had the great honour of going on the BBC's 'The One Show' as a part of coverage of their Coronation Dish competition. I went as someone who had voted for a recipe made by a fantastic chef called Claire Lara, which was a King Oyster Mushroom Filo Tart. It was a truly delicious recipe, with mushrooms, butternut squash, and lots of fantastic spices wrapped in coiled up filo pastry. Highly recommended. Claire herself was an absolute delight too and I remain chuffed to bits to this day that I got to stand alongside her.

The coiled filo thing I later learnt was borek, a pastry dish that comes from the eastern end of the Mediterranean, including the Balkans, Greece, Turkey and beyond. There are lots of different fillings including lamb, feta, and spinach. The concept lends itself to many other things.

As a great fan of filo, I've consequently adapted and made my own. This one is based around my family's tastes and has a nod to Claire's amazing dish with similar spicing. But I strongly recommend looking hers up too!

I eat this with salad, and it is a special lunch.

Serves 4, with salad on the side.

Ingredients

Glug olive oil
1 onion chopped
300g butternut squash, cut into chunks
200g chicken mince or leftover chicken meat
500g frozen spinach, defrosted and excess water drained / squeezed away
200g feta cheese, crumbled
4 cloves garlic, minced

LIFE FOOD

2 teaspoons medium curry powder
2 teaspoons turmeric
Salt & pepper
Fresh coriander and parsley chopped
3 sheets of filo pastry
Melted butter and sunflower oil mixture with cinnamon mixed in
Chopped mixed nuts

Method

First make the filling. Roast the butternut squash chunks in the oven, on a baking tray, at 180° C / 350° F / Gas mark 4, for 30 minutes.

In a suitable sauté pan or saucepan, over a medium heat, warm the olive oil, and cook the onion to tender but not browned. Add the chicken mince or the leftover chicken and cook for a few minutes, then add the garlic and the spices. When the chicken is cooked through, take it off the heat, add the spinach and combine thoroughly, and mix through the butternut chunks, squishing them into the mixture. Season the mixture and allow to cool for a few minutes until it is no longer hot. Lastly, crumble the feta cheese into the mixture and mix lightly to combine. Don't let the feta melt into the mixture, keep the chunks whole as much as possible.

To make up the borek, you need to get the filo pastry laid out. I give detailed guidance on how to handle filo pastry in the recipe for Salmon and broccoli filo quiche in the Mains section, so refer to that if needed.

You want all three sheets fully buttered with the cinnamony butter mixture and laid out on top of each other, but in a way that they half overlap lengthwise giving you a total area of laid out pastry that is twice as long as a single sheet, and the same width. This will be roughly 60-70cm long and 25cm wide. This is so you have a borek that coils sufficiently.

THE ABLE DIABETIC

Once the filo is laid out, working along the edge of the long edge, spoon the filling mixture out evenly all the way so that you have a neat and regular length of filling. Then roll the filo, one long edge towards the other, so that it encases the filling, and so that you end up with a long sausage, 60cm long.

Then take an end of the sausage, hold it in place, and wrap the length of the sausage around it to give you the coiled structure of a borek.

Transfer the borek gently onto a greased baking by sliding it gently, supporting the coil. Brush it with any remaining butter mixture and sprinkle the chopped nuts liberally over it.

Then pop it into the oven which needs to be at 180° C / 350° F / Gas mark 4, and bake it for 35-40 minutes until it is golden and crispy.

When it is cooked, allow it to cool slightly before you transfer it to a serving plate or board. Serve warm.

LIFE FOOD

Chickpeas with Indian-spiced stir-fried greens

I found this recipe in the book 'The 8-week blood sugar diet recipe book' by Michael Mosley's wife Dr Claire Bailey, when I was actively on the lookout for recipes that featured lentils. This has both lentils and chickpeas. I actually didn't think it sounded that inspiring but having made it was pleasantly surprised. It is filling enough, substantial, and yet quite delicate. It is something quite unlike most other things in my repertoire. It's also quick, so it can be made for lunch in a short time. I have, as usual, adjusted the recipe slightly.

Incredibly sadly, we lost Michael Mosley in 2024. My heart goes out to his family most of all, and all the colleagues and friends who knew him personally. I, like many other people who only knew him as a broadcaster, nonetheless felt incredibly sad about his untimely death. His contribution to peoples' health has been simply immense. I include this partly as a way to mark his impact and as a sign of gratitude.

It also goes without saying that the book this is taken from, is an excellent and imaginative reference for anyone wanting to be healthier, so is highly recommended.

This recipe is designed for 2. Double the quantities for 4.

Ingredients

1 tablespoon rapeseed oil
1 teaspoon mustard seeds
1 large onion, diced
2 fresh chillies, preferably green diced
1 teaspoon turmeric
½ 400g tin of lentils
½ 400g tin chickpeas
500g green cabbage, shredded
1 teaspoon garam masala
Salt to taste

Method

Heat the oil in a large sauté pan and add the onions, mustard seeds and chopped chillies and cook gently, stirring them, for a few minutes.

Add the lentils, chickpeas and cabbage to the pan and increase the heat, cooking for about 7 minutes, stirring to stop anything from sticking. The dish is cooked when the cabbage is still bright green but just tender.

Sprinkle the garam masala and salt over and serve straight away.

LIFE FOOD

Roasted butternut and red lentil pâté

It was Jamie Oliver who first made me think about squished butternut making a good basis for a hummus dish in his book Save with Jamie. It is my favourite book of his, a genuinely practical book that I have actually used quite a lot. In the main, however much I enjoy reading a cookbook, I make on average less than 1 of the actual recipes, so this book stands out.

In it, he suggests roasting a butternut when the oven is on for another reason, to save energy (great idea) and then to use the resulting cooked flesh for a number of different things: squash fritters, squash hummus, squash sauce for pasta, and squash bruschetta. This is inspired by the hummus idea and made my own.

I have a real tendency when faced with having to concoct a quick meal to eat either cheddar, or maybe peanut butter, on toast or in a sandwich. It's not a great default. I can do better.

An alternative is hummus, so it's great if that's in the fridge. I love hummus. I love butternut squash. I prefer butternut squash when it has been roasted in chunks. The orange makes me go to red lentils. Somehow all of those influences have evolved to this inviting and yummy concoction which is great in lots of ways.

Ingredients

¼ of a butternut squash 300-400g, cut into largish chunks
100g of red lentils, rinsed
Garlic, 2 cloves, minced
2 tablespoons extra virgin olive oil
Juice from half a lemon
1 teaspoon smoked paprika
1 teaspoon cumin
30g soft cheese e.g. Philadelphia
Pinch of salt

THE ABLE DIABETIC

Method

Roast the butternut squash in an oven at 180° C / 350° F / Gas mark 4 for 40 minutes (or do as Jamie does, and roast the flesh of the whole thing when you're cooking something else and just use the flesh you need for this recipe).

Put the red lentils into a saucepan of boiling water and simmer for 30 minutes until soft and squishy. Drain.

Its best to make the pâté while the lentils and the butternut chunks are still warm as they combine best with the other ingredients this way.

Put the lentils, roasted butternut, and all the other ingredients in a food processor, and whizz until fully smooth. Check the seasoning.

Scoop out, and place in a suitable serving dish, then put in the fridge to chill until you are ready to eat. This is great with seeded crackers, sticks of celery, and granary toast.

LIFE FOOD

Spanish tortilla

I think my mum used to make 'Spanish omelette' when I was very young, but I remember the words rather than the food. Maybe I didn't eat it because I struggled with eggs during my childhood. Hated is more accurate actually.

These days I think the way they use eggs in Spanish cooking is wonderful. The highly flavoured garlicky eggs with lots of gutsy peppers and tomatoes is a fabulous dish.

In the main, when you talk about Spanish tortilla you would traditionally expect it to contain quite a lot of potato too, the waxy kind, in little nuggets. Many recipes omit the peppers and tomatoes entirely. The adaptation I make is to reduce the amount of potato considerably, and increase the other vegetable ingredients, although I'd be happy to add in some potato depending on circumstances.

The word 'tortilla' can be confusing. In some contexts, it means the flat, sometimes corn based bread used to make burritos and enchiladas, and in others this egg based dish. They are different.

A tip too for making this recipe. To get the tortilla to be fully cooked through, especially at the top, the pan you make it in either needs to go under the grill or in the oven, so the handle has to be OK for doing that.

This recipe serves 4 with salad, bread etc. on the side.

Ingredients

1 onion (brown or red), chopped
4 cloves of garlic, minced
A decent glug of olive oil
1 red pepper, deseeded and cut into small chunks
1 green pepper, deseeded and cut into small chunks
2 large tomatoes, deseeded and cut into small chunks

THE ABLE DIABETIC

1 medium potato, waxy type, cut into small cubes – optional
8 eggs
Salt & pepper

Method

In a large, good quality frying or sauté pan, with a handle that won't melt or burn when exposed to the oven or grill, warm the olive oil to a medium heat and add the chopped onions to the pan. Cook for a few minutes until translucent but not brown.

Add the garlic and peppers and continue to cook at medium heat until the peppers are tender but not scorched. At this point add the tomatoes and continue to cook for about a minute or two. If you are using potato, it needs to be cooked before the peppers, and takes longer than the rest of the vegetables, so don't add the peppers and garlic until the potato cubes are tender.

Meanwhile, break all the eggs into a separate bowl, season with the salt and pepper reasonably generously, and whisk together so that they're combined. Don't over whisk as this affects the texture.

Once the tomatoes have been cooking for 2 minutes, use a spoon to mix all the vegetables around so they are evenly distributed, and pour over the egg into the pan shaking it slightly to get the egg to settle around everything.

Reduce the heat under the pan to low, and cover the pan, because you want to cook the egg right through, and in order to do this, you want the middle cooked before the part touching the pan risks burning.

When the egg is set and the top is almost cooked, either put the whole pan into the oven (if the pan can take that) for just a few minutes at about 160° C / 325° F / Gas mark 3, or heat the grill and finish it off under that.

LIFE FOOD

Leave the tortilla in the pan for a few minutes after cooking so that it cools and solidifies a bit. When it's ready, loosen it with a palette knife around its edges, and then put a plate or a board on top of the pan, and tip it upside down carefully, so that it's on the board.

THE ABLE DIABETIC

Provençale mixed lentils and grains

A food innovation over recent years has been these pouches of rice and grains that you can get in the supermarket. They are ready to eat mixed grains of various sorts, usually with a particular cuisine theme of some sort. Merchant Gourmet, Jamie Oliver, and supermarkets themselves make them.

I'm afraid that I'm a bit judgemental in this zone because when I see a pouch I see plastic in landfill forever, and that seems pretty unnecessary to me for what is basically a cup of some of the most basic food products there are. But parking my eco-arguments, I see that they are a ready source of healthy food for people who otherwise might turn to much less healthy ready food, so I'll try and be reasonable.

My approach is to basically copy the producers, and make my own 'mixed grains'. It's not hard to identify the grains / rice / lentils used and the flavourings added. This is cheap, healthy, and has far less packaging waste.

One I turn to a lot is this Provençale style recipe. This is less of a family recipe and more something I make for myself. I would typically make the batch at the weekend and then use it over 4 meals. Just like you'd use a pouch, you can use this alongside some salad, with a simple omelette, or even on its own for a simple and easy lunch. The family are more than happy to eat it as part of a salad.

I encourage you to experiment with this concept. You can take whatever mixture of grains you fancy (red rice, brown rice, bulgur wheat, freekeh, red lentils, puy style lentils, green lentils, chickpeas, etc.) and flavour them with Mexican style spices, north African, Indian...

Some lettuce, tomato, cucumber, carrot and a spoonful of these grains makes a perfect diabetic lunch.

LIFE FOOD

Serves 4 / makes 4 portions.

Ingredients

Glug olive oil
1 red onion, chopped
4 cloves garlic, minced
2 sticks celery, chopped into small dice
2 medium carrots, chopped into small dice
½ 400g tin of chopped tomatoes
100g (total weight) of mixed lentils and rice, made up of 25g red lentils, 25g lentilles vertes (puy style), 25g green lentils, 25g brown basmati rice
2 teaspoons of a combination of dried thyme, rosemary, tarragon, oregano (although fresh is even better)

Method

In a small to medium saucepan, heat the olive oil to a medium heat on the hob, and add the red onion, garlic, celery and carrot. Sauté for a few minutes until translucent. Meanwhile boil a kettle of water.

Wash the mixed lentils and rice in a sieve, and add to the saucepan, mixing up with the sautéed vegetables and pouring on enough water to cover plus a centimetre extra. Add the tinned tomatoes, and sprinkle over the herbs. Keep at a low simmer for 30 minutes, adding more water if it is needed, and when you test the rice and it's cooked, take it off the hob.

You can eat this hot, warm, or cold. It's delicious all ways.

If you're going to keep it in the fridge, where it will last for a few days, you should get it in as soon as it is a bit cooled down for food safety reasons.

BAKES

BAKES

Soda bread

Potato bread

Flapjack

Apple and Caerphilly cake

Sarah at number 3's fruitcake

Date butter squares

Lemon and poppy seed cake

Clementine cake

LIFE FOOD

While this is a book about eating well as a type 1 diabetic, it is also a book, I hope, that is about eating well for the soul too. What I want most is to put food on my family's table that gives pleasure and is health-giving. In that context, I wouldn't dream of not including things I bake, even though I myself have to be sparing about eating them.

I often bake a cake at the weekend that gets eaten over the week. It might be one of the recipes here, but it is just as likely that it will be a Victoria sandwich with jam and butter icing, because that's Greg's favourite. My favourite, in case you're asking, is coffee and walnut cake made by Lauren. She is a gifted baker. She uses the same recipes as I do but her results are always lighter and have a certain something extra special.

Occasionally I wonder if it's a bad thing that cake is around. Fairly quickly I conclude that I would far rather my family were eating homemade cake than something industrial, full of preservatives and emulsifiers, and wrapped in plastic that they've picked up. And I hope that the love that goes into the cake is irreplaceable too.

All of the bakes included in this section have earned their place. And have proven to be manageable for me and good for our way of eating. Generally, the breads get made as a special component of an otherwise lighter meal at the weekend. The cakes benefit from fruit and seeds. Flapjack is an essential in my life, so it's here! None of these things are 'bad for you'. Even if you're a t1d.

THE ABLE DIABETIC

LIFE FOOD

Soda bread

I was taught how to make soda bread by my goddaughter Áine's dad, Ivan when we visited them in Ireland. He knocked some up in no time at all, and warned us that it was delicious and would disappear in moments. Oh, my goodness how right that was. Still-warm soda bread spread with good butter is a hard to beat. So, we brought this recipe back to England with us.

From a practical perspective it is a grand thing to have in your repertoire, because it is amazingly quick from start to finish, and the perfect accompaniment to some soup. The speed of preparation is down to the fact that there is no yeast involved and so none of the leaving, kneading, proving stages that go into making 'real' bread. The bread is dense as a result, and super satisfying.

Prior to learning this recipe, I always thought that to make something with buttermilk you had to get the ingredient specially, so it was a revelation to learn that buttermilk is easily made with standard milk to which you've added the juice of a lemon. The acidity thickens the milk up in a few minutes.

The ingredients for this are always to hand: we always have wholemeal flour, milk, and lemons in the house.

So, it's true that this is satisfying. It is also true that this is a slightly dangerous food for me to have around because it is incredibly moreish, and the density of the bread means that it is wall to wall carbs. I can eat it, but only in small quantities. It's therefore best served alongside something that doesn't otherwise contain carbs. Having said all that, I would be bereft not to have this in my life.

Makes a medium round loaf.

THE ABLE DIABETIC

<u>Ingredients</u>

450g wholemeal flour or a wholemeal / plain flour mix
1 teaspoon salt
1 teaspoon bicarbonate of soda
450ml buttermilk
(Make the buttermilk with 450ml of milk and the juice of a lemon)
If wanted, a tablespoon of treacle or a tablespoon of honey

<u>Method</u>

Pre-heat the oven to 200° C / 400° F / gas mark 6.

In a large bowl, combine all the dry ingredients: flour, salt and bicarbonate of soda.

If you are using, add the treacle or honey.

Pour on most, not all, of the buttermilk and bring the dough together. Add the remainder if the dough is too dry and you need it to bring it together. Using your hands, press and squeeze the dough into a ball.

Liberally dust a clean worksurface with flour and transfer the ball of dough over. You don't need to knead this at all, just press it into an even, domed shape. Then transfer it to a floured baking tray, and cut a deep cross (2cm deep) across the top of the dough. Transfer the tray to the oven.

Bake the bread for 45 to 55 minutes by which point it will be higher, browned, and the cross will be there, but the dough will have risen into the cuts.

This is ready to eat as soon as it has cooled a bit, and is fantastic eaten fresh. That said, a piece of day old soda bread toasted and buttered is similarly gorgeous.

LIFE FOOD

Potato bread

So, I remember that the advice is not to make this when you're on a diet! It is something that you could easily eat more of; it's delicious. Which is why it doesn't get made that frequently, and when it does, it is as a planned accompaniment to an otherwise straightforward vegetable soup, containing minimal carbs. Also, my portion needs to be a maximum of one slice of the bread. So, either factor a few people in when you're making it, or at least a couple of young growing ones who will run off a large slice!

All of that said, food should be a pleasure to eat, and this truly is. Soup and this bread make a feast. Serving this elevates the simplest meals.

The main recipe has a couple of alternatives too, both courtesy of Delia, and both delectable as well.

Makes 1 loaf (6 people)

Ingredients

110g goats' cheese, cut up into small chunks
4 spring onions – sliced
150g potato
Tsp fresh thyme, chopped
175g self-raising flour
1 tsp salt
1 egg
2 tablespoons milk
1-2 tsp grain mustard

Method

This bread can be baked as soon as you make it, so you can get the oven on and warming at the start if you want to serve this soon.

THE ABLE DIABETIC

The oven needs to be pre-heated to 190° C / 375° F / Gas mark 5.

You'll also need a baking tray that you have greased.

Start with a large bowl and put the flour and salt into it. Then peel the potato, and coarsely grate it straight into the bowl. Add the chopped spring onion, thyme, and two thirds of the chopped goats' cheese. Mix all the ingredients up together.

Put the milk and mustard in another smaller bowl, and add the egg to it, then beat together. Pour this into the larger bowl with the flour mixture and squeeze it all together so that it forms a dough. Don't work it hard, it just needs to be made into one mass, but you don't need to knead or in any way mess with it.

Flour a board and transfer the dough onto it, then using your hands, shape the dough making it smooth and round and regular. Transfer this to the prepared baking tray.

Press the remaining cheese into the bread, and if you have any spare thyme sprigs, press them in too.

Pop the baking tray into the hot oven, and bake for about 45 minutes, by which time the bread should look golden brown. Bring it out of the oven and transfer to a wire rack and allow it to cool.

The bread is amazing when it is served still warm. It needs absolutely nothing to go with it!

Alternatives on the theme, both well worth making:

- Feta cheese, potato and rosemary
- Parsnip, parmesan and sage

LIFE FOOD

Flapjack

Most of my early cooking was done at Mum's side, when she was baking. I helped make cakes and quiches, not proper food so much, but lots of bakes.

It was part of the curriculum to do Home Economics at school when I was 11, and I think that's where I made flapjack. I was terrible at Home Ec. I had a bad attitude because I thought it was a waste of time, and I often didn't have the right ingredients nor the preferred basket to bring said ingredients into school. I also think that we just didn't make things that were particularly nice or useful. In fairness, flapjack is both nice and useful.

Since it is made with oats, although flapjack is a treat, it is at the end of the baking spectrum which is healthier for a t1d, and I would say flapjacks definitely have their place in our lives. For example, if I go on a long hike, flapjacks are my food of choice as I walk.

These are basic flapjacks and great as they are. The most unusual flapjacks I've had were laced with black pepper and dates, and were amazing if you fancy trying that!

Ingredients

275g butter
275g golden syrup
300g rolled porridge oats

Method

You'll need a 20cm x 20cm baking tray greased and lined with greaseproof paper.

Preheat the oven to 160° C / 325° F / Gas mark 3.

THE ABLE DIABETIC

Put the butter and golden syrup in a saucepan, and put it on a medium heat on the hob, to melt entirely. Don't let it get so hot it is beyond melting though. Remove the pan from the heat and stir in the porridge oats until they are thoroughly coated in the butter and syrup mixture.

Transfer the oaty mix to the baking tray and, using the back of a wooden spoon, flatten the oats down until fully smoothed into the corners of the tray, and level. Put in the oven and bake for 35-40 minutes until golden.

Take out of the oven. While they are still warm, in the tin, score the lines to cut the flapjack into squares, and then leave to go fully cool. Once cooled, cut where scored fully, and make into flapjack squares.

LIFE FOOD

Apple and Caerphilly cake

I first made this recipe about 25 years ago, and recently found it written down on a scrap of paper. I remember both thinking at the time that it sounded intriguing and probably pretty nice. I'd never seen cheese as an ingredient in a cake before. This is not, in case it's unclear, a 'cheesecake' in the classic sense at all. It is a cake that has cheese in it! My weakness for cheese was surely the decisive factor the first time I made this. It's unlike anything else.

I'm including it because although it has plenty of 'bad' things like oil, and white flour, it also has a lot of apples, as well as nuts. From a t1d point of view, dried fruit isn't brilliant, but combining it with fat, cheese (protein), and nuts is a different proposition. All up, I think there's a lot of good delivered by this cake as well as a few things that need to be taken in a measured way.

Ingredients

175g self-raising flour
1 teaspoon baking powder
75g light brown sugar
100g mixed fruit (raisins, sultanas etc.)
100g mixed nuts
575g eating apples
2 eggs
90ml sunflower oil
225g Caerphilly cheese

Method

You need a 23cm cake tin for this, well-greased. Springform is best because the cake is quite crumbly.

Pre-heat the oven to 180° C / 350° F / Gas mark 4.

THE ABLE DIABETIC

Put the dry ingredients, flour, baking powder, and sugar in a large bowl and mix. Add the mixed fruit and nuts, the sugar, and mix again.

Wash the apples, then peel, core, and slice finely. Add these slices to the bowl and mix again. Then beat the eggs and the oil together, pour over the ingredients in the bowl, and stir to combine well.

You're now ready to assemble the cake in the baking tin. Put half of the mixture in the tin, and press down so that it's level. Cut the cheese into thin slices. The cheese is crumbly so don't be surprised if this is a bit messy, and don't worry. Lay / sprinkle the cheese on top of the levelled cake mixture. Then add the rest of the mixture and again, press it down gently and level it.

Put the tin in the oven and bake for 50 minutes to an hour. It should be firm and browned.

Take it out and leave in the tin to cool. This is important because the cake is a bit of a delicate thing!

After the cake has cooled down, you can carefully remove it from the springform tin and put on a plate (or a wire rack). It is delicious to eat while still warm. Otherwise, treat as a normal cake.

LIFE FOOD

Sarah at number 3's fruit cake

At the time we moved into our street, now over 15 years ago, a couple of other families did too. All of us have families with one boy and one girl, similar in ages, the three of us mums are all called Sarah, and each of us started our careers in accounting. Both other Sarahs are great neighbours, proactive in helping people, and also great fun.

Many years ago, Sarah at Number 3 gave me this recipe for turning fruit that is just slightly past its best into cake. I'm pretty sure this is exactly her recipe because I wrote it down at the time in my special book. I've used it a lot. It's a brilliant recipe to have to hand because it's so practical. It delivers on its promise. It works.

I've said before that fruit isn't a huge thing for me, and although Jim gets through a lot of fruit, it isn't rare for there to be some fruit around that has got beyond the point anyone will find it appealing. From a food waste point of view, this is an excellent thing to have to hand.

From a health and t1d point of view, yes this is cake, and so treat with care, but it is cake with fruit and the fibre that comes with it, so have one slice, savour it fully, and enjoy!

The cake keeps reasonably well, but the fruit's moisture can make it a little susceptible to going mouldy, so get your non t1d friends and family to help eat it up.

Ingredients

800g of finely chopped, past-its-best fruit such as pears, apples, plums, peaches, berries
150g soft butter / equivalent e.g. Stork
150g caster sugar
300g self-raising flour
2 teaspoons baking powder
2 large eggs

THE ABLE DIABETIC

<u>Method</u>

You need a 25cm cake tin, greased and preferably lined with greaseproof paper.

Pre-warm the oven to 180° C / 350° F / Gas mark 4.

In a large bowl, cream the butter and sugar together until light.

Add the fruit. I should note that the fruit needs to be chopped up fairly small, and remove cores and seeds, but don't worry about the skin. It's good to keep the fibre! Once the fruit is in, blend it all together until well-mixed and creamy.

Add the flour, baking powder, and eggs, and mix together until fully incorporated. Transfer the cake mixture to the prepared tin, smooth it down, and pop it in the oven.

Bake for about 1 hour, until it is risen, springy to the touch, and a skewer inserted into the middle comes out without any wet batter on it.

LIFE FOOD

Date butter squares (Mum's recipe)

My mum is a good baker and made all her own food when I was a young child. I was born in Zambia, where my parents had moved as soon as they got married and, because ingredients were not available consistently, she had to be resourceful. The ingredients here are fairly basic, but the recipe is spectacular.

Of all her recipes, I've chosen to include this because it is a top favourite from my memories of childhood. I haven't adapted it at all, and make it only in a blue moon, because it really is too tempting. I suppose I'm including it here partly because I want it recorded for posterity, but also because even though I think I'm quite liberal about the way I handle my t1d, there are plenty of things that are so heavily carb-y they're over the line of acceptability. This is certainly close to the line! However, it makes me downhearted to think something so loved is banned from my life, and so it isn't. Also, there are a lot of dates in this, and they have a lot to recommend them nutritionally, and so it's not all bad!

This is transcribed from Mum's handwriting, which is why I've included the imperial measures. This makes 24.

Ingredients
Pastry:
10oz plain flour [280g]
8oz marg or butter [225g]
Filling:
3oz butter [85g]
3oz soft brown sugar [85g]
12oz stoned dates, chopped [340g]
1 level tablespoon plain flour
¼ level teaspoon ground cinnamon
1 level tablespoon golden syrup
Caster sugar

THE ABLE DIABETIC

<u>Method</u>

You need a Swiss roll tin 12" x 8" [30cm x 20cm]

Make the pastry. Sift the flour. Using the coarsest side of a grater, grate the butter into the flour and stir it through with a knife. Mix in sufficient water to make a fairly stiff dough, then wrap the pastry in greaseproof paper and leave it in a cool place.

Put butter, brown sugar, chopped dates, cinnamon and syrup into a pan over a low heat, bring the mixture to the boil, stirring all the time. Simmer it for a few minutes then remove the pan from the heat and leave to cool.

Divide the pastry in half and roll one half into a rectangle to line the base and sides of the tin. Use remaining pastry for the top. Damp the edges of both pieces of pastry with water and firmly press together. Mark the top of the pastry into diamonds with a knife. Sprinkle liberally with caster sugar.

Bake in the centre of oven at 200° C / 400° F / Gas mark 6 for 15 minutes then 180° C / 350° F / Gas mark 4 until golden brown.

Leave to cool then cut into pieces.

LIFE FOOD

Lemon and poppy seed cake

When I was at school in the USA, I lived in the Residential Community or "RC". There were 14 of us, supported by teachers who lived on site or came in to help. One of those teachers was Jamie, who taught Chemistry, and also two courses that I took, one on evolution, and the other on scientific thought. Over thirty years later, Jamie remains one of my most favourite people. She embodies kindness, integrity, and the pursuit of fairness. I don't know anyone who has lived more closely to their own ideals nor who has continued to push the boundaries of what a person can achieve so assiduously. She is much loved. She helped with cooking for us at the RC, and it was her lemon and poppy seed cake that has somehow come to remind me of her in the years since. Jamie was sustainably minded long before it became fashionable, and she chose sound food options because she understood why it mattered.

I love the fact that the lemon flavour and the poppy flavour mingle so well. They're so distinct on their own, and very much have their own identity. But combined they blend so nicely and make each other somehow better. Sums up Jamie.

There is a question about whether to add a light icing or not. Obviously it involves sugar to do so, and there is no question that it is unnecessary. The cake is great without. What slightly nags at me is that it is only the zest of the lemons in this recipe that is used and that troubles me. If the lemon juice will be used for something else, then great. But lemons don't last without their skin and so if they're going to waste, make the light drizzle icing.

Serves 12

Ingredients

225g butter
225g caster sugar
4 medium eggs

THE ABLE DIABETIC

225g self-raising flour
1 teaspoon baking powder
2 tablespoons poppy seeds
2 large lemons, zested
2 tablespoons of milk

If making icing:
The juice from the two lemons
70g icing sugar

Method

This recipe requires a loaf tin, 1 litre volume, about 16cm long x 11cm wide. Prepare your loaf tin by greasing it and lining it with greaseproof paper.

Preheat the oven to 180° C / 350° F / Gas mark 4.

In a large bowl, cream together the butter and sugar until it is light and fluffy, and then add the beaten eggs gradually, beating with every addition. You can do this by hand or use a handheld electric whisk.

In a separate bowl, combine the flour, baking powder, and poppy seeds. Again, gradually add a spoonful of the dry mixture to the main bowl, and keep beating it in. Then add the lemon zest and the milk and mix them well in. You should have a smooth and quite wet batter.

The next stage is to transfer the batter to the prepared loaf tin, and smooth it over.

Put the loaf tin in the oven, and bake for 45-55 minutes. The cake is ready when you can insert a skewer and it comes out clean, showing the cake is fully cooked through.

Let the cake cool down, first in its tin, and then on a wire rack.

LIFE FOOD

To make the drizzle icing, in a small bowl, get the juice of the lemon and stir in the icing sugar until fully combined and dissolved. It will still be very liquid. Make some small cuts or incisions with a sharp knife or a thin skewer into the cake and gently and slowly pour the icing evenly over the surface, hopefully in a way that means some of the icing seeps into the cake. Allow to dry. It will leave a lemony crust across the cake.

Clementine cake

It was Jim's mum, Margaret, who made this cake. She was a splendid cook as well as being a lovely lady, and one of her hallmarks was the production of at least 3 desserts per meal at family gatherings, and then the encouragement for all of them to be tasted by everyone!

She made this specifically for me when I was having allergy issues and had discovered that a wheat protein was the underlying cause. Without the baking powder this is a flour and gluten free recipe. (And yes, I do have an unusual allergy, but fortunately it's under control now).

Again, it's a bit of a special recipe because of the inclusion of ground almonds in place of flour, and although it's quite a sweet thing to eat, the nuts help with the glycaemic index profile, and you get the benefit of the clementines and the nuts, so it's not 'cake as we know it'. I have also reduced the sugar a bit which doesn't make any difference as far as I can tell.

I don't include it here because it's 'healthy'. I include it because it is delicious, unusual, and special.

The recipe, as I understand it, is a Nigella one, itself based on a Claudia Roden one, which hails from Spain and Portugal region originally. Apparently, it can be made with the same weight of any citrus fruit, in the same way.

Serves 8

Ingredients

4 clementines
6 eggs
200g white sugar
250g ground almonds
1 teaspoon baking powder

LIFE FOOD

<u>Method</u>

This requires a 20cm springform baking tin. Grease and line it before you start.

The first stage involves the clementines, and I would point out that you do not do anything except wash the fruit before you do the first stage. There is no peeling. Start by putting the clementines in a saucepan, with some cold water, and bring to the boil, then simmer for an hour and a quarter. Drain the water away and allow the fruit to cool completely. Cut the clementines in half and remove and discard any pips. Put all the remaining fruit, including skin, in a food processor and process until smooth.

Separately, in a large bowl, add the eggs, sugar, almonds and baking powder and beat together until well combined. Transfer the clementine pulp to this mixture and stir in well.

Pour the cake mixture into the prepared tin. Cover the top of the tin with foil and put in an oven heated to 190° C / 375° F / Gas mark 5. After 40 minutes remove the foil. The cake is ready when a skewer inserted into the middle comes out clean.

Remove from the oven and allow to cool fully within its tin.

This is a cake that will improve if left for one or two days.

DESSERTS

DESSERTS

Raspberry and apple pie

Baked apples

Deconstructed Black Forest

Tropical crumble

Cranachan

Yogurt, banana and brown sugar trifles

Poached pears

It's a myth that a type 1 diabetic can't have pudding. In fact, this is one way that I think being a type 1 diabetic is easier than being type 2. I'm not type 2 and so don't speak with experience of it, but I do know that managing your blood glucose is much more about what you eat being highly controlled, whereas a type 1 can adjust their insulin doses. If I decide to have dessert, I simply inject some more insulin to meet the carb-load involved.

I say 'simply', but it's not as simple as that. A dessert has the dual risk or downside of (a) involving extra carbs and (b) those carbs being typically high on the glycaemic index and thus causing a fast peak in blood sugars. As with all food, to manage it well you need to understand it, and then make sensible choices for you.

When I eat dessert, I make sure I enjoy it!

At home I don't make desserts often, but there are times when the occasion calls for one, and then I do it my way.

The principles that underpin my approach here are just easy things that make a difference. First up, it's better to have a sweet thing after a meal, than as a standalone item. After a meal, especially if it is vegetable and fibre-based, your stomach is already digesting, and this impedes the absorption of the dessert's sugary carbs. Eating the dessert as part of a meal means you're just adding to a meal glucose peak, rather than adding a standalone one, for example if you were to have a slice of cake in the mid-afternoon. So that helps.

It also helps if the dessert has got something high fibre factored in. Add oats, or use some wholemeal flour, or use nuts and seeds. I am a big fan of crumble because the crumble can be made healthier with the addition of oats and seeds.

Also, base the dessert around fruit. I've said before that I don't eat loads of fruit, and this is because it does come with an increase to blood glucose. However, fruit is good for you, and contains other nutrition besides carbs. So, building the dessert around fruit means you are getting the benefit of the fruit's vitamins and fibre.

Different fruits have different levels of carbohydrates. Berries in particular, as well as apples and pears, have lower levels and are a good choice. The less the fruit is pulped and processed, the better too. Let your body do that work, and the impact on your blood glucose will be reduced.

These principles have influenced the sweet things we eat after meals, and despite adaptations, no one thinks of them as 'not dessert'!

LIFE FOOD

THE ABLE DIABETIC

LIFE FOOD

Raspberry and apple pie

This is my Gran's. Or at least the closest I can get to her's without actually having the recipe. I have a strong memory of it though, and that's a great thing to guide me. What do I remember about this? The pastry being thin and crisp. The raspberry filling being richly dark, vibrantly pink, and sweet. Quite a lot of sugar added to this. It was made in a glass dish. Oblong and quite deep. Generous. I wish I had that dish. Goodness knows where it ended up. I'm grateful I have the memory, which is clear and detailed, and takes me back to a place that was very warm and loving.

This many raspberries is a real luxury. I know this has apples in it, but they're playing second fiddle. This dish is all about the raspberries. From my t1d point of view, the raspberries are a great base fruit. About 12% of the weight of raspberries is carbohydrate, so not a lot at all. A good start!

I've experimented and think that the apple is best being something like a Cox apple. Bramley's make the filling too fluffy, when it's meant to be glossy. You want something that breaks down a bit but is complementary to that sweet glossiness.

Serves 4-6

Ingredients

500g raspberries (or equivalent frozen, defrosted)
2 dessert apples, Cox style
50g sugar

Pastry:
200g plain flour
25g sugar
Pinch salt
75g lard / butter mixture

THE ABLE DIABETIC

<u>Method</u>

You need an ovenproof dish about 20cm x 15cm, and 1 litre volume.

Preheat the oven to 180° C / 350° F / Gas mark 4.

Peel the apples and discard the peel and core. Chop the apples into small pieces. Place them in a small to medium saucepan on a gentle hob, with the raspberries and the 50g sugar. Cook for about 5 minutes.

Transfer the cooked fruit into the ovenproof dish.

In a largish bowl, place the flour, pinch salt, and 25g sugar. Add the lard and butter, 75g total combined weight, and cut into cubes. Using your fingertips, rub the fat into the flour until you have regular breadcrumb texture. Then pour cold water gradually onto the breadcrumbs and press together with a knife until the pastry dough all comes together. Don't overdo it.

Briefly squeeze the pastry together and just slightly work it. This is unusual for pastry, but I find gives the texture I'm after.

Roll out the pastry onto a floured board until it is a regular thickness of about 2mm, which is quite thin. Place the pastry over the dish and press it down around the edge, ideally with a fork. Make some holes in the top of the pie with the fork too, to allow steam to escape.

Bake this in the oven. I suggest putting the ovenproof dish on a baking sheet because if any of the filling does seep out of the edges of the pastry it will make a real mess of the inside of your oven! It will take between 25 and 35 minutes depending on your pastry.

Give it a little moment to cool before serving as the filling will be absolutely piping hot.

LIFE FOOD

Traditionally, my Gran would have served this with clotted cream that she had made herself. A bowl of the unctuous fruit, a slice of the crisp and delicious pastry, and the lusciousness of clotted cream. She served with a combination of her precision and generosity. That completes a beautifully happy memory.

Baked apples

As made by my Mum. This takes me back to my teenage years, and the quantities of food produced by Mum for a large family: 4 children to feed! I have often thought about that when I'm feeding my own family – it's a lot of work. This is a good dessert for a crowd because you obviously just provide one apple per person, and they're all popped in the oven together, so it's a great one for groups.

This dessert may be simple, but it is also good for you, and comfortingly enjoyable. This is a time-effective way of providing a pudding that delivers a sense of being home.

As with everything in this chapter, I'm not saying that this recipe is something that you can just abandon diabetic principles over; there are carbs. But, the serving is essentially an apple, and although adding both raisins and sugar increases the carb count, what you're eating is well worth factoring into your carb and insulin amounts for a meal.

I always use Bramley apples for this. They are the queen of cooking apples, and I love their fluffiness when cooked.

Serves 4

Ingredients

4 largish Bramley apples
40g raisins
20g brown sugar
1-2 tsp ground cinnamon

Custard to serve

LIFE FOOD

Method

Get an ovenproof dish that the apples fit into snugly. Pre-heat the oven to 180° C / 350° F / Gas mark 4.

Wash the apples and, using a corer, carefully remove the whole core. Try to make sure that none of the fibrous woodiness of the core stays behind. Then, using a paring knife, score a line in the skin all the way round the "equator" of the apple, halfway between both the bottom and top holes.

Place the apples in the dish they will cook in.

In a small bowl, mix the raisins, sugar, and ground cinnamon together well, and then, using a teaspoon, carefully put ¼ of the raisin mixture into each apple.

Put the dish in the oven and bake for 30-40 minutes. Test by gently putting a skewer through the largest one to check that it is soft and cooked through.

Serve straight away.

Deconstructed Black Forest

This is a cool way of delivering dessert. We're quite used to savoury food being served in a 'buffet' or 'mezze' style way. The same principle doesn't generally apply in the dessert zone. As this recipe shows, it can be quite brilliant to do this.

This deconstructed black forest came about because I wanted to make a black forest cake for Jim's dad on a special occasion, but that posed challenges. Greg hated cherries then, and still isn't keen now. Lauren gets eczema which we were discovering was due to cows' milk, and so she was avoiding it at the time, which meant the cream was problematic. Both liked chocolate cake! And then of course, there's me to think about. The full thing is pretty heavy duty on the sugar front.

But, by separating the components of the pudding into a cake part, a cream part, a chocolate sauce part, and a cherries part, you create a mix-and-match situation where people can assemble what they want. It worked marvellously well! Everyone was happy.

For me, my serving is a small cube of cake, some cherries, a bit of sauce and some cream, which combines to be a super-special treat. You'll note too that I use only dark chocolate here and that's because it inherently consists of lower sugar than milk chocolate.

Our favoured 'cake' element has evolved to become chocolate brownies. My preferred recipe for them comes from the Hummingbird Bakery cookbook which contains a lot of sugar, so I meant it when I said my portion size is a small cube!

Serves 8

LIFE FOOD

Ingredients

Brownies:
130g dark chocolate
120g unsalted butter
200g caster sugar
85g plain flour
2 eggs

Sauce:
150g dark chocolate
25g butter
125ml double cream

400g Fresh cherries, stoned

300ml Double cream, whipped

Method

You need a baking tray that is about 20cm x 20cm and deeper than 2cm for this. Grease it and line it with greaseproof paper. This step is essential because the brownies have so much sugar in them that they tend to stick.

Preheat the oven to 170° C / 325° F / Gas mark 3.

Start by melting the chocolate and butter for the brownies. Put in a heatproof bowl and either do this 'bain marie' style, by putting the bowl above a small saucepan of simmering water on the hob (making sure the bottom of the bowl is a decent distance from the water), or in the microwave where you heat for 20 seconds in the heatproof bowl. Stir the chocolate until it is completely smooth.

Take the chocolate off the heat and add the sugar to the bowl, stirring it well into the chocolate. Then add the flour in one go, and stir in. Lastly, break the eggs into a bowl, beat them to mix up the whites and yolks, and then add to the chocolate bowl and mix in well. You will have a thick, gloopy mixture with a glossy appearance.

Pour or spoon the chocolate mix into the prepared baking tray and put into the oven. Bake for 30 minutes and check. The amount of cooking the brownies get determine their texture. If you cook too long they will be cake like. Too short a cooking time and they'll be overly wet. You're aiming for fudgy, which is when the top has a crust, and the edges have gone quite crunchy, but the middle is still soft.

Let the brownies cool in their tin fully before lifting out of the tin and cutting into squares.

To make the sauce, in a similar way to how you make the melted chocolate for the brownies, put the chocolate in a clean glass bowl with the butter and melt until smooth and runny. Then add the cream and mix to combine fully.

Serve the brownies alongside the cherries, whipped cream, and warm chocolate sauce allowing people to build their own.

Tropical crumble

This recipe is from an old Cranks book, which I dug out to see if the way I make it is actually the recipe. It isn't! Mine has evolved over time! The inspiration is completely theirs though. I did enjoy re-reading that when this was on the menu, crumble orders tripled, which isn't a surprise.

The key to this recipe is its unusual fruit to topping ratio. The crumble is just a sprinkling that adds texture but doesn't remotely overwhelm the fruit. I love it because although it has carbs from the fruit, the emphasis is on fruit and not added sugar. It's also made into something quite special with the addition of the rum or brandy.

Serves 4-6

Ingredients

1 fresh pineapple (about 1kg weight)
1 large orange
100g raisins / sultanas
25g desiccated coconut
1 dessertspoon rum or brandy
1 teaspoon fresh ginger, minced

100g flour
100g oats
100g butter, cut into small cubes

Method

Preheat the oven to 180° C / 350° F / Gas mark 4.

Prepare the pineapple: cut off all the exterior green stuff, and then quarter lengthways and remove the woody central core. Cut the flesh that is left into cubes. Put the flesh into a saucepan, with the raisins or sultanas, coconut, ginger, and rum or brandy, and simmer gently for 5 minutes.

Allow to cool slightly and transfer to an ovenproof dish.

In a separate bowl, put the flour then the oats, and add the butter, then rub the butter into the flour and oats until you have a fairly even chunky breadcrumb texture and no butter lumps.

When you are ready to put the crumble in the oven, sprinkle the crumble mixture over the fruit in the ovenproof dish. There isn't that much crumble, so rather than evenly spread it, I like to make it a bit more haphazard so there are chunkier bits. Also, it is best not to leave the crumble topping on the fruit for long before cooking as it can get soggy that way. You're aiming for crispy and crunchy.

Put the dish into the oven, and cook for 40 minutes until the crumble topping is golden and crunchy.

Eat immediately. I don't think this needs any cream or custard.

LIFE FOOD

Cranachan

This recipe is dedicated to Jim's father, Alastair, who sadly is no longer with us. He had Scottish family roots and after he died we decided to start a tradition of holding a Burn's Night supper at home, at which we eat haggis, drink whisky and read aloud the Robbie Burn's poem that was read at his funeral. It's a lovely way to remember him.

The meal ends with cranachan which is a Scottish dessert, and which is a pretty good choice for a diabetic, not too sweet, with oats and cream in the mix. There's a little bit of effort involved in putting it together, but it is well worth it!

Some of you might prefer to abandon my layering. A more random mixing of the ingredients in the style of an Eton Mess is a much quicker way of preparing this. And go for it if that works for you. In my view there is something uniquely enjoyable about the layers and how you experience them when you're eating the cranachan.

Serves 4

Ingredients

300-400g fresh raspberries
100g rolled oats
350 ml double cream
75ml whisky (Scottish would be best!)
3 heaped teaspoons honey, preferably heather honey

Method

Making the cranachan involves preparing the three parts: raspberries, toasted oats, flavoured cream, and then assembling them. So, the first stage is all preparation.

THE ABLE DIABETIC

Pick through the raspberries and clean off anything you don't want to eat. Handle them with great care. You want raspberries that are intact and undamaged. Set aside.

Measure out the rolled outs and then sprinkle them evenly all over a baking tray. Heat the oven to 150° C / 300° F / gas mark 2 and put the tray in the oven. It won't take long before the oats start to toast – they will darken. It is important that you get them to the golden stage and not beyond when they will taste burnt rather than nutty. So, watch them closely. Also, taking the tray out part way through and mixing the oats around a bit helps to ensure that they are evenly toasted. The smell by the way is gorgeous. Let them cool completely.

The last preparation part is the make the flavoured cream. In a sufficiently large bowl to allow for the cream's expansion, pour the cream in and whisk until thick, either with a handheld electric whisk or by hand. Pour on the whisky and spoon in the honey and continue to whisk until the cream is fully whipped, but hasn't turned.

You're now ready to assemble the cranachan. Don't start to do this unless all the component parts are cold.

I use individual drinking glasses for this, by which I mean short 'lowball' glasses because I think they look great.

My aim is to construct this in the following layers: cream, oats, raspberries, cream, oats, cream, which means dividing the cream into 3, and the oats into 2. Then, share each of those parts among the glasses. Try to do this gently so that the different elements don't combine too much, because ideally the oats will stay light and crunchy up until the point of eating. If they're squidged into the raspberries or the cream, they start to absorb moisture. It's a delicate operation! Once made, the individual glasses should be put in the fridge until they are eaten. They'll happily sit for a few hours.

I promise you it is worth the trouble!

LIFE FOOD

Yogurt, banana and brown sugar trifles

Simple this one. Almost not quite a recipe, more a simple assembly. And usually, the ingredients are close at hand. Surprisingly yummy. Yes, there's sugar and fruit in it, but it can be easily adjusted so that a diabetic gets one with amended ratios of yogurt to sugary stuff. The layer of sugar develops into a fudgy layer if you leave it in the fridge for a few hours. Works brilliantly.

Serves 4

Ingredients

500g Greek yogurt (or other plain kind)
2 ripe but not over-ripe bananas
7-10 teaspoons of dark brown sugar e.g. muscovado

Method

You need 4 glass containers for this, each that can hold 300ml.

Peel and slice up your bananas, and lay the slices in the bottom of the 4 glass containers, sharing them out in an appropriate way (a bit less fruit for the t1d).

Spoon over the yogurt and smooth it so that it's flattish.

Carefully sprinkle the dark brown sugar gently over the top of the yogurt. The t1d should have only 1 teaspoon. The rest, double that. Leave the dishes in the fridge for a couple of hours before serving. The sugar will become a sticky, melted, toffee-like layer.

Poached pears

My fondness for pears has turned up before. I'm not sure that I prefer any fruit over a perfectly ripe pear, eaten just as it comes, with the juice at its peak. Pears provide a great basis for dessert too, and I could happily write about chocolate cake with pears, and pears in an almond sponge.

But poached pears are a beautiful thing, much more elegant than my food usually is.

You can poach pears in white wine, red wine, even perry or cider and there are recipes which do without the alcohol too. I like the dimension alcohol brings. You also see a lot of recipes with spices of many kinds which are also nice. This recipe though leans towards just lightly complementing the pears' own flavour, and is fresh and slightly aromatic.

Most people would probably serve with cream. You don't have to.

Serves 4

Ingredients

4 very firm (not ripe) pears that are all the same size
200ml white wine
120g sugar
1 large lemon, juiced and finely zested
2 star anise

Method

Start by making the syrup. Put the wine, sugar, star anise, lemon juice and lemon zest in a solid bottomed saucepan over a medium heat and stir until the sugar has dissolved. Bring gently to the boil and let it cook for 5 minutes so that the liquid has slightly thickened.

Meanwhile, prepare the pears. Carefully peel them so their shape is retained, and leave the stalk on at the top. Cutting a slice off their bottoms will help them stand up on a plate at the end.

Place the pears in the saucepan with the liquid, and put the lid on. You want them to simmer and poach for about 30 minutes. Don't move them around, except for once mid-way through cooking, when they should be turned over. Towards the end watch them carefully and when they look to be tender, check by inserting a sharp knife. It should go in smoothly.

Take the pears out of the liquid and sit on a plate to cool. The syrup will thicken into a syrupy liquid as it cools. If it looks too wet, simmer it a little longer and then let it cool. Once it has cooled and thickened, pour over the pears and serve.

A SPECIAL MENTION

A SPECIAL MENTION

Pear and date chutney

LIFE FOOD

Pear and date chutney

At our house, number 2, where we moved when Lauren was 2, and I was pregnant with Greg, the garden was a horror of gravel and paving, with only one lovely thing: a gorgeous pear tree, maybe 30 feet tall. I loved it from the start and now have lots of happy memories associated with it. One, for example, is of a gorgeous April day when it was loaded with white blossom and Lauren had her 5th birthday party pinata hung underneath; I remember the crowd of little girls in the dappled sunshine all squealing with joyful laughter as the pinata came open and showered sweets out.

The quantity and quality of the pears we get varies every year, but there are a lot. Early on I knew that they would largely go to waste unless something was made of them that would last, and so began the pear chutney tradition. Every year, many jars are made, all with their own personality.

Chutney is a great condiment - a little goes a long way, and the extra dimension brought to a sandwich, ploughman's, or curry is something we enjoy.

Once you get going with making chutney you quickly learn that the essential recipe can be readily changed via swapping out one thing for an equivalent. I am quite cost conscious and find it painful to use expensive wine vinegar in these quantities, so I have settled into using ready-spiced malt pickling vinegar. While I still make things up as I go along, the recipe below has evolved into my 'standard'.

One important note: I use a massive pan for this with a 12 litre volume. The chutney takes a good lot of bubbling away, starts quite volatile, and gets sticky at the end, so it's good to have a pot that can accommodate the experience!

When you are dealing with boiling hot jars, lids, and chutney there is scope for danger, so be exceptionally careful and ensure pets and children are not under your feet.

THE ABLE DIABETIC

Makes about 20 jars.

<u>Ingredients</u>

3kg pears
2.5kg onions
750g dates (block)
Red birds' eye chillis
Chilli flakes
1 garlic bulb
1 litre malt pickling vinegar
700g sugar

<u>Method</u>

This will make about 10lbs of chutney, so have enough glass jars and lids (can be second hand / mixed sizes) to take all of it.

Start by prepping the pears: wash first. I no longer peel them, but I do leave the core and pips behind for the compost. Chop the pear flesh into roughly 1-2cm dice. Having a combination of ripe and underripe pears works well, as does having different size dice. Some will melt completely into the chutney while the less ripe will contribute to the texture.

All of the pears go into the pan.

Next step is dicing the onions. You don't want the skin, nor the tops and tails. You want fairly small dice. Once chopped, pop all in the pan.

At this point, pour over the vinegar and stir in the sugar, and put on the hob to warm up. You want to get it to a gentle simmer, and while it is warming, stir fairly frequently to help dissolve the sugar and to stop anything sticking and burning. Once the sugar is dissolved you can just leave the pot with minimal attention for the hours of cooking it will need.

LIFE FOOD

All that's left is to add the other flavourings. I like to see the flecks of the birds' eye chillis, so I cut them slightly largish on the diagonal and keep all the seeds intact. We like our spice, so I also add a fairly generous sprinkling of chilli flakes, maybe a heaped teaspoon, which is a lot! Prep the garlic by taking off the papery outer, and slicing the cloves. You could crush or otherwise prep if you want, but the look of the little triangles in the chutney is nice I think. Again, a whole bulb might sound a lot but in this quantity of chutney you'll like it I'm sure.

The addition of the dates adds flavour, sweetness and body to the chutney. Its best to buy dates in the baking blocks, and chop them roughly into small chunks about 1cm wide.

All those flavourings get chucked in the pan, and then all you have to do is bubble, stir from time to time, and watch it closely for the changing stages.

What starts as a very liquid and quite pale looking pan full will steadily thicken and get darker, glossier, and then slightly stickier. For a long time (like 1.5-2 hours as a rough estimate) it'll need little stirring, but once it starts to catch on the bottom of the pan, you need to be stirring quite frequently. It's good to be doing something else in the kitchen through this last stage so you can regularly check in on the chutney.

The last, critical, stage of the chutney making is bottling it. I found this scary when I first started.

The first thing is to have a set of glass jars with tightly fitting lids that are scrupulously clean.

When the chutney is ready, I put all the glass jars on a baking tray (with a lip so they won't roll off), on their side, and put them in the oven which I then heat to 160° C / 325° F / Gas mark 3 for a few minutes. At the same time, I put all the lids into a saucepan of boiling water and boil for 5 minutes.

THE ABLE DIABETIC

You can NOT touch anything with your own fingers so have tools assembled nearby. I use tongs and a serving spoon both of which have been sterilised in the pan of boiling water.

The final stage is to bring the jars out of the oven and use the tongs to put them all upright. Position the saucepan of boiling chutney near the jars and carefully, spoon by spoon, fill the jars. Don't worry if you drip chutney on the outsides, just leave it, but try to be tidy.

Once the jars are all full, or you have run out of chutney, put the saucepan out of the way, and bring the lids in their pan of boiling water closer. Using the tongs, place the right lid on the right jar.

The final stage is to tighten the lids to close and seal the jars, which I do with a tea towel to protect my hands from the boiling heat. Then leave. To the greatest extent possible, leave alone until fully cooled. At this point you can wipe down the jars of any spilt chutney on the outside, making sure not to break the seal.

All done except for polishing and labelling. Remember to put the date on the labels! Then store in a dark place.

You can eat the chutney straight away, but I like it to mature for about 3 months before opening.

The jars of chutney will last for a long time unopened. We've eaten chutney which is a decade old! And once opened, the vinegar will protect it from things growing on it so it will keep well to eat for a long time too.

BIBLIOGRAPHY

Abensur, Nadine, *The New Cranks Recipe Book*, Phoenix Illustrated, 1997
Bailey, Dr Clare, with Schenker, Dr Sarah, *The 8-week blood sugar diet recipe book*, Short Books, 2016
Dutta, Krishna, *The Dal Cookbook*, Grub Street, 2013
Lawson, Nigella, *Nigella Express*, Chatto & Windus, 2007
Malouf, Tarek and The Hummingbird Bakery, *The Hummingbird Bakery Cookbook*, Ryland Peters & Small, 2009
Oliver, Jamie, *Save with Jamie*, the Penguin Group, 2013
Slater, Nigel, *Real Fast Food*, the Penguin Group, 1993
Smith, Delia, *Delia Smith's Complete Cookery Course*, BBC Books, 1995
Smith, Delia, *Delia's How To Cook*, BBC Worldwide Ltd, 1998
Smith, Delia, *Delia Smith's Summer Collection*, BBC Books, 1996
Various contributors, *Good Housekeeping Cook's Year*, BCA (Ebury Press), 1995

INDEX

Antipasti 36
Apple and Caerphilly cake 247

Bacon and lentil soup 52

Baked apples 270
Bean burgers and sweet potato fries 143
Beef and black bean noodles 170
Beetroot and goats' cheese salad 199
Bloody Mary tomatoes 32
Borscht 64
Broccoli and cannellini bean soup 50
Butternut squash and feta salad 197

Carpenter's pie 151
Carrot and nut salad 189
Chickpeas with Indian-spiced str-fried greens 225
Clementine cake 256
Coleslaw 195
Cranachan 277
Crudites 28
Curried split pea soup 57

Date butter squares (Mum's recipe) 251
Deconstructed Black Forest 272
Dhal plus plus 99

Fattoush 187
Filo carrots 34
Flapjack 245

Gish's lentil quiche 127
Green mac 'n' cheese 157
Griddled asparagus, pear and goats' cheese salad 201

Halloumi kebabs and brown rice 154
Homity pie 112
Hummus 30

Kedgeree 148

Lamb and lentil moussaka 160
Lauren's cayenne chicken farfalle 138
Lemon and poppy seed cake 253
Lentil and apricot soup 47
Lentil and mushroom Bolognese 83

Mackerel and tomato pasta 136
Mediterranean chicken borek 222
Mexican bean soup 60
Mexican eggs 96
Minestrone soup 54
Moroccan aubergine couscous 116

(Nigella's) noodle salad 191

Pakoras 102
Pea, lemon and chicken risotto 88
Pear and date chutney 287
Peppered mackerel pâté 211
Pesto cod, mash and green vegetables 107
Pho 69
Poached pears 280
Potato bread 243
Provençale mixed lentils and grains 232
Puy lentil, feta and red pepper filo pie 167

Rainbow noodles 130
Raspberry and apple pie 267
Ratatouille 109
Roast aubergines, chickpea mash and harissa 172
Roast chicken and green salad 85

Roasted butternut and red lentil pâté 227
Roasted peppers 213
Roasted nuts 27
Roast jeera cauliflower and carrots 105

Salmon and broccoli filo quiche 122
Sarah at number 3's fruit cake 249
Sausage and borlotti bean casserole 140
Seared tuna, cannellini mash, roast tomatoes and olives 174
Smoked haddock and sweetcorn chowder 67
Soda bread 241
Spanish tortilla 229
Spicy Ricey 146
Spinach and brown rice bake 133
Stuffed mushrooms 216
Sweet potato and feta parcels 164
Sweet potato enchiladas 118

Tabbouleh 185
Tropical crumble 275
Turkish red lentil soup 62

Vegetable crumble 92
Vietnamese rice wraps 218

Waldorf salad 193

Yogurt, banana and brown sugar trifles 279

AND WITH GREAT THANKS

A great many people have played supporting roles in the genesis and writing of this book.

A long time ago Jamie German's example of filling her life with books and absorbing their knowledge inspired me to put reading and learning at the heart of life; her's was an invaluable example, among many others which she showed me. Now, this "Able Diabetic" endeavour takes me a step further as I pass my own knowledge on. I'm so grateful to Jamie for being at the heart of my life for so long.

I was originally motivated to write about my experience of living as a type 1 diabetic by Fiona Shanley, who I had the immense privilege of working for a few years ago. Aside from being an extraordinarily brilliant executive, she is one of the most generously spirited people I know. In a conversation about someone grappling with a new type 1 diagnosis, she suggested my experience could be broadly valuable to others, and from that comment my writing started. Thank you Fiona, for everything.

I know my grandmothers, Gran and Nan, would be thrilled to see this book. Though very different to each other, they were both family-orientated, made the best of everything no matter how humble, were excellent cooks, and always made me feel loved. Sadly, they are no longer with us, but their spirit is, and remembering them and their impact makes me feel profound gratitude.

I have been fortunate over the years to receive support from many doctors, nurses, and other health professionals. Over the last decade, Michelle Hooper has been my primary advisor, providing support, guidance, and a sympathetic ear. As a specialist Diabetes Dietician, her knowledge has been helpful to me, but more than that, I appreciate her always kind and supportive manner, which is ever present.

Food has always been central to my enjoyment of life, but never just the food: always the people I have been breaking bread with, whether family, friends, colleagues, or beyond those categories. To everyone, thank you for the patience you've shown me when I've been dealing with insulin, checking blood glucose levels, and resolving hypos. I have always known that alongside your companionship, you are also providing your moral support. Above all, thank you for sharing your time with me.

I have been growing a collection of cookbooks that is 300 strong since my early twenties, and I owe those food authors thanks for sharing their thoughts. It's been interesting to note in the writing of this book whose recipes have become stalwarts of my repertoire. Specific writers get mentioned along the way in my book, and its bibliography shines a light on the ones with specific impact, but I'd like to add my sincere thanks to all for the sheer pleasure that reading their words has given me over the years.

As I have been working towards finally getting this particular dish to the table, support from key people has really mattered. Tone Sarjanen, thank you, you got me laser focused on getting this out! My dear friend Becky Rafferty, your wise words as we walked along Dorset clifftops were hugely useful and clarifying. In the final production stages, it has been Jim's technical support and detail focus, Lauren's proof reading, and Greg's ever present encouragement despite GCSE exams that have got this book done!

I live this life, which does come with a side order of the ongoing, sometimes irritating, always constant thought and work that goes into managing diabetes with my partner Jim, and our beloved children, Lauren and Greg. This book is not just my Life Food, it is also their Life Food. They have been with me every step of the way.